GRANNY'S
POETRY

GRANNY'S POETRY

One Young Girl, Her Poetry, and
the City That Grew With Her

CHARLES ALLUMBAUGH

Farmhouse
Publishings

I wrote this book as a way to leave something behind for my grandchildren and great-grandchildren to remember me by. Over time, it has grown into more than I ever imagined. My hope is that it helps them understand where they came from and feel a deep sense of pride in their heritage.

I dedicate this book to my beloved wife, Doris, and to our children, Chuck and Dana.

TABLE OF CONTENTS

FROM THE PEN OF
CHARLES ALLUMBAUGH
CLASS OF 1958

Granny's Poetry

When I first decided to write this book, I was going to give a little history of my grandmother, quote a few of her poems, then give a little of my history, and quote a few of my poems. But as I got into what I thought was going to be a "little" history, I realized how much of her life and her parents' lives was the history of Dallas itself.

My grandmother's history actually begins before her birth, but we will get to that in a little bit. She was born May 20, 1874, not long after the Civil War ended. She was my grandmother: May Belle Cox Allumbaugh.

Several years ago, I found a small paperback book where my grandmother had written 89 poems between the pages. The book was published as a *Pocket Almanac Account Book*, and was an advertisement for Brown's Iron Bitters, which purported to cure many ailments such as headache, constipation, and biliousness. The book also served as a calendar for the years 1889 and 1890. On the opposite page was a place for a memorandum, and this is where she had written her poems. It was hard to date exactly when she wrote the poems and entered them in the pages of the almanac, but it seems she would have been about 15 or 16 years old.

Nearly all of her poems are very similar in that they are very short, only four lines long. There are a few exceptions, and one of the exceptions is a two-line poem. It is quoted here and is one of my favorites.

76

In the golden chain of friendship
Regard me as a link

While many of her poems are just musings of a young girl, some are really thoughtful and have a lot of meaning. The numbers above each poem correlate to how she had them numbered in her journal. I did not include every poem from her little book, and so I kept the numbering system she had in order to keep track, so I would not repeat one later in the book.

As you read through my grandmother May Belle's poems and the surrounding history, I hope you are inspired to find the stories and history in your own family. There's always so much more under the surface, and it is fascinating to find out all of the layers of the story.

MY GRANDMOTHER'S HISTORY

39

Think of me now
Think of me ever
Think of the fun
We had together

Her dad, my great-grandfather, Hartwell Bolin Cox, was born January 22,1840, in Greene County, Illinois, and died January 26, 1918, in Rylie, Texas. He is buried there in the Rylie Cemetery.

Her mother was Luthary Ann Moore Cox, born October 18, 1845. She married H. B. Cox when she was 22 years old. She died January 28, 1879, at the young age of 33. She is buried in the Long Creek Cemetery, Sunnyvale, Texas. Her grave marker was made from the wood of a Bois d'Arc tree. There are several wooden markers that could have been her grave; I was unable to determine the exact marker.

H. B. was married four times and outlived all his wives. He had a total of 14 children. He and his first wife, Luthary Ann Moore Cox, had seven children. He and his second wife, Margaret Ann Moore, had one child before her death in November 1890. His third wife, Nancy Hurd, had one child before her death in 1893. He then married Lethe Ann Spears. Together, they had five children before her death in 1916.

H. B.'s mother, Anna Hunnicutt Cox, brought him and two brothers, James Michael Cox and Davis B. Cox, to the Dallas area around 1844. No one knows for sure what happened to H. B.'s father, William Bolin Cox. Several stories have been told about his demise.

Three of the stories are as follows:

1. One story says that early settlers took up a collection and sent William B. Cox and others north for supplies. They disappeared and were never heard from again. Some think that Indians killed them.
2. Another belief was that William Bolin Cox was a school teacher in Illinois. When the family moved to Dallas, William traveled back and forth to teach school. He died on a trip coming back to Dallas.
3. William died in Illinois before Hartwell was born.

When his parents first came to Texas, they settled where the city of Dallas is now located, at or near the present site of the old courthouse. In 1861, he moved to Rylie, which remained his home. Some in the family believed that the land was given to the city of Dallas to be used for a Courthouse, and if it was ever used for another purpose, it would then revert back to the family.

32

The sea is wide
The water is deep
And in your dreams
I hope to sleep

30

Forget me not
Forget me never
Till the glittering sun
Sets forever

FAMILY TIES TO THE CIVIL WAR

22

When rocks and hills divide us
And you no more I see
Just take a pen and paper
And write a line to me

My great-grandmother received several letters written from the battlefield in Arkansas from at least two Confederate soldiers asking her to wait for them to return. I still have several of the letters. More than one of the letters was signed by David Peters. I have not been able to show a relationship to Wm. C. Peters of the Peters Colony.

The Peters Colony had control of several types of land grants. The Republic of Texas gave the Peters Colony over one million acres of land directly for performing, promoting, and surveying services. Thirteen settlers within the Peters Colony city limits were given 640 acres for each head of family or 320 acres for each single man.[1]

There were also headright grants issued within the city of the Colony. The Constitution of 1836 gave all heads of families living in Texas on March 4, 1836, 4,605.5 acres and single men over seventeen years of age 1476,1 acres.[2]

Wm. C. Peters was a trustee of the Texas Emigration and Land Company. At one time, they were given control of more than ten million acres. That contract was signed by Sam Houston on July 26, 1842. They were responsible for bringing settlers to North Texas and dividing up the land for all that met the requirements. There were several requirements, including meeting the definition of a family. A family would be eligible to receive 320 acres. "Family" was understood to mean a man and his wife with or without children, a widow or widower, with two or more children under the age of seventeen years. Or, if all girls, they may be over the age of seventeen years. Males over seventeen years of age were entitled to 160 acres of land if the surveys were paid for before emigrating, or 120 acres if paid for by note after settling on the grant.[3]

There were costs involved in executing the notes. The resident agent would receive $15. And the single man would pay $7.50 for the cost of the survey, payable 12 months after the date, with interest to maturity of the note — the certificate in such a case will be issued by the agent.

These requirements and costs were from an advertisement for "Emigration to the Trinity & Red River Colony."[4] The complete advertisement was about two pages long.

Another letter was signed by H. D. Beckner. He is quoted in some files from the Antietam Institute about his history in the Civil War. These files are from different Confederate soldiers called "Reminiscences of the Boys in Gray, 1862-1865." His statement of his part in the war is as follows:

HENRY D. BECKNER, Cleburne, Texas–was born April 8, 1839, in Cass County, Mo. Enlisted in the Confederate Army January 15, 1862, At Dallas, Texas, as a private in Company C, Eighteenth Texas Cavalry, under Col. Darnell's Regiment. I served in the Trans-Mississippi Department, under Col. R.S. Baggest of Missouri. In July, 1862 we were dismounted at or near Little Rock, Ark. On August 28, 1862, I was detailed to repair wagons and later on was sent to Little Rock and placed under Captain Ped, Quartermaster during the winter of '62 and '63 until March, when I made coffins for those of our soldiers who died in hospitals. On the 16th of May, 1863. Was then transferred to Captain Johnson, Quartermaster. And went to Fulton, on the Red River, where we remained till April 4, 1864. Was then transferred to Col Bogges of Missouri. On the 20th of May, was given a furlough and went to Dallas.[5]

I found this interesting since I have a couple of letters written in his handwriting to my Great Grandmother while he was in Fulton, Ark. One letter is dated February 6, 1864. He is also asking her to wait for his return.

H. B. was wounded and returned before either of them, and married her while he was home. I can't help but wonder if he had not been wounded, would I even be here today?

The Civil War

Abraham Lincoln had several reasons to get us into war with the Southern states. His legacy includes: preserving the union, ending slavery, and working toward civil rights and social equality. Ending slavery was very important to him. I cannot help but wonder if he knew how many thousands of young men would die on both sides of the war, would he have tried to do it peacefully instead of the war between the States?[6]

The American Civil War actually began on April 12, 1862, when Confederate troops opened fire on Fort Sumter in Charleston, South Carolina. The Union Forces surrendered less than 34 hours later.

The Battle of Bull Run is often called the first battle of the Civil War. While it may have been the first major battle, it was not the first battle.[7]

Sixteen days before, there was a smaller but very important battle that took place in Missouri. This was the battle of Carthage that took place near Carthage, Missouri, with both sides claiming victory. [8]

Union troops led by Colonel Franz Sigel went against Missouri Governor Claiborne Fox Jackson. Jackson has the distinction of being the only state Governor to ever lead troops into battle.

Jackson had 2,600 Infantry troops and about 1,500 Cavalry troops, but they were poorly equipped. He also had another 2,000 volunteers who were completely unarmed. He did have seven cannons at his disposal. Jackson sent these volunteers to the rear to keep them from being slaughtered. Sigel was outnumbered, but he had 1,100 well-trained German-American troops. He also had eight cannons. He believed that his disciplined, well-equipped troops could carry the day.

Sigel formed a line and ordered his troops to advance the half-mile or so and engaged the enemy. Before he reached the main force, he encountered the rebels' forward skirmish line commanded by J.O. Shelby. Shelby moved his 150 men between the two opposing lines. This was only a small action, but it gave Jackson time to attack Sigel. Sigel was able to break through Jackson's lines and make it to Carthage, where he stayed the night. He had suffered 44 dead and wounded. Jackson had lost 74 dead and wounded. Jackson was the victor, but Sigel claimed victory because he came away from a much larger force and was able to escape.

Southerners called it the Battle of Manassas, and the Northerners called it the Battle of Bull Run. On July 21, 1861, the Civil War began in earnest.

Senators from Washington, D.C., and civilians from the surrounding area gathered near Centerville, Virginia, to watch the battle. Some even brought picnic baskets.

The Confederate army had shelled Fort Sumter in April 1861. The Congress complained because the Union troops did not retaliate in kind. There were rumors that Abraham Lincoln was trying to forge a compromise with the South.[9]

They wanted a quick campaign to show their superiority in battle, and Abraham Lincoln was under a lot of pressure to do something. The Battle of Bull Run was it.

The Union Army did well in the morning of the battle, but as evening came, the tide was turning. The Union troops saw the writing on the wall. Around four in the afternoon, the Union generals started calling to retreat. The soldiers started fleeing, and it was over for the Union. President Abraham Lincoln was stunned, and members of Congress were shocked, and it was obvious that the war would not be an easy win.[10]

I had not wanted to get into a story about the Civil War because that has been done over and over. I did find it interesting, though, how the first couple of battles began, and it seemed that Lincoln just let it get away from him. I still believe he did not intend to let it go as far as he did.

I do believe that states' rights were important to the Southern states, but the main right they wanted was to be able to own slaves. The only good thing to come out of the war was the end of slavery. The sad part is that after 160 years, there are still hard feelings between the races.

H. B. COX CIVIL WAR JOURNAL

40

I love you long
I love you well
I love you more
Than tongue can tell

In between the first and the last battle of the Civil War my
great-grandfather, Hartwell Bolin Cox, kept a journal of his time
in the war between the states. I am using his version of the war in
between the first and the last battle.

He and his two brothers, Christopher Cox and David B. Cox,
served in Company B, 19th Texas Cavalry, Nat M. Burford's Reg-
iment, under Captain Allen Beard.

He titled the journal *Camp Wright: Civil War Diary*.

A cousin of mine, Helen J. Thompson-Sullivan, a great-grand-daughter of H. B.'s had possession of the diary, and in 1972, she transcribed it, trying to keep it authentic by not correcting the spelling. I have included some excerpts here. What you see is what you get, poor spelling and all. Sharon Bryant of West Texas, currently has the original diary. Sharon is the granddaughter of H. B.'s last child, Polly Josephine Cox.

I find it amusing that some of the atrocious spelling he used was because he spent many years after the war as a reporter for the *Mesquiter* newspaper. If I use direct quotes from the journal, I will write it just as he did. Remember, much of this was written while he was on the battlefield under horrendous circumstances.

This was Camp Wright

We marcht to Red River in Red River County and campt from August the 8th, 1862 until August 31st. Then we marcht into Arkansas to Camp Davis on or near the washitaw River, not far from Camden. There we staid from Sep the 12 to the 20th from thence to Camp Ship-lan on the north side of the Arkansas River oposite Little Rock wher some of our boys died. We arived Sept the 26th.

Here we remained until Oct the 15th. Here I saw the first rail rode and cars that I ever saw. My brother James was sick at Little Rock. We marcht from north or north east to Camp Hope where we arrived Oct the 16th. Here we saw some of our old neighbors and also relation that belong to another regt. Hear I saw General Holms (and the notorious Col. Sweet riding his bobtail horse. We march from hear on the 21st of Oct east to Desarc on White River. We arrived on the 22nd. Hear my brother Davis was taken sick. I staid hear with him with a number of others from our regiment. Our regt Crost White river and march east and crost Cash River and thence to Cotton Plant. One of the lowest marchest sicklayest country in all Gods creation. I remained in Desarc som days wher I went to camp to procure mules and a hack to take my brother to Cotton Plant. When I told my business I was not permited to return too my sick brother but as good luck would hav it my brother that was left sick in Little Rock got well enough to travel. He came to Desarc and found Davis sick. There meeting was an affecting one. After some little skimmishing betwen some of our regiment and the federals, we returned to Desarc on the 20th of November. While campt hear we received clothing from home. It was on the 28 of November. It was about that date that we caused to lament the death of one of our Lieutenanrts, Joseph Johnston. His short career was the most brilliant one in our company. I, being a particular friend of his, lost no time in informing his fond wife by letter of his death. — Lake Bluff

November the 30th we marcht down White River to or near DeVallas Bluff on the Memphis and Litle Rock rail rode. While campt here there was some trouble that arose between our regt and General Haws. He escaped without any violence from us. I was taken sick here on the 5 of December but nothing serious. About the last of December I tuck the mumps.

January the 3rd, 1863 I was sent up, White River on a boat by the name Tom Sugs to Desarc. I went aboard about 10 oclock in the day and then locomotion of the boat being vary slow and she was laden heavy and the trip up, stream and owing to the repeted sheling of corn over the negro deck hands heads by the mate, we landed in Desarc about 10 at night. The voyage being about 20 miles, I thought we did well. Here I found my sick brother. Here I remained in the hospital and in the convalescent house until 17 of January.

Here I will break away from the Diary and talk about the *Tom Suggs* that H. B. went up the White River on.

The *Tom Suggs* was a sixty-two-ton side-wheel steamboat built at Cincinnati, Ohio, in 1860. The vessel was ninety-one feet and eight inches long and twenty-two feet and five inches wide. In 1862, Captain John W. Dunnington armored it with cotton bales and mounted an eight-inch cannon on its bow to be used against Major General Samuel R. Cyrtes's army of the Southwest.[11] It is not believed that the *Tom Suggs* actually saw any action during this time, but it was used by the Confederacy to haul goods up and down the White and Red Rivers.

On August 9, 1863, Brigadier General John Wynn Davidson's Cavalry approached the town of Clarendon on the White River. The *Tom Sugg* and the *Kaskaskia* were the last two Confederate steamboats operating on the White River and were docked at Clarendon. On August 12, bolstered by the 32nd Iowa Infantry, steamed up the White River in pursuit of *Tom Suggs*. The *USS Cricket*, one of three naval ships, broke away from the *Lexington* and the *Mamora* at the Red River and continued in its pursuit of the *Tom Suggs*. It caught up with the *Tom Suggs* and boarded the vessel and returned it to Clarendon. The *Tom Suggs* was refitted as a tinclad gunboat, and on August 16, it was armed with a 12-pounder rifled howitzer, the ship being used as a transport.[12]

The *Tom Suggs* was later taken to the U.S. Naval Base at Cairo, Illinois, where she was outfitted with two 24-pounder howitzers. The name was changed to the *Tensas* and was commissioned at Mound City, Illinois, in January 1865, where she served the remainder of the war on the Mississippi River.[13]

It was decommissioned on August 7, 1865, and sold at public auction for the sum of $6,200 to E. B. Trinidad of New Iberia, Louisiana. She was renamed the *Teche* and was sold again to the Attakapas Mail Transportation Company.[14]

The *Teche* (*Tom Suggs*) was wrecked in Bayou Teche in 1868.[15]

Back to H. B.'s Diary

About the 8 or 10th our regt was ordered to the Arkansas post but too late. The federals took that post on the 11th of January. The federals came up White river to Des Arc with a gun boat. Myself and brother Davis and some others of our company all of which were convalescents left about the time the gun boat landed. There was snow and ice on the ground. We didn't try at Camp Shiplap Long. Hear at Litle Rock one of my cousens died. NOTE: (H. B. had at least three cousins by the name of Beeman in his company. It may have been one of them. It was a Beeman that married John Neely Bryan, Founder of Dallas.)

After seeing my brother on a boat for Pine Bluff, we marcht for the same place through mud and water from one to too feet deep. We campt below Pine Bluff on Read Fork. Hear I was sent low down on Read Fork near the Missisipi River on the courier line. Hear I remained until some time in April. While I was hear the federals came out on top Read Fork. Hear I will make mention of the Lieutenants name that was in command of the courtier line. His name was Triplet, a young man fond of adventures and rite hear he had the pleasure of one as well as my self. It was way in Feb that the federals came up Read Fork on the west side. We being on the east side. One Mr. Smith lived som 2 or 3 hundred yards below whear we was stationed on the same side of the fork. As the feds came up the fork—to me it looked like 6 thousand—Mr. Smith being below a log or tree, the feds could not see him. They opened fire on him with small arms and canon but never got his rang. He says he shot several. The deep creek separated them or of cours they would a got him.

About this time Lieutenent Triplet crost the fork in a canoe and finding a servant over there that belong to some of our men, he borrowed his horse and went down the fork to get a sight and shot at the feds and he got both.

Our men, of course had hid the ferry boat at the crossing whear we was stationed. The lieutenant as soon as he fired, he made his way back to the bank opisit where me self and 3 others were anxious awaiting his arrival. When he came he made no halt but rode in to the bayou. His horse would not swim. He floundered about back to the same side he started from. We sent a negro boy to him with the canoe. He (the lieutenant) got in the canoe and they had got started good when to add to his adventure, the canoe being vary small, it was capsized, The Lieutenant made his way back to the same side of his embarcation. Hear he stript him self all to shirt and drawers and made a safe trip, and I thought a cold one, to our side by swimming well. His pants. Boots, hat, and coat way on the other side of his adventure, The canoe in the middle of the bayou. We procured a long pole and after som trouble we brought the little craft to land. No one would under take the voyage after the Lieutenants wardrobe. After putting out a watch for the feds, who was bvy this time as we supposed on their march up the bayou and not far off as we afterwards found out, I with a small bord for a paddle under tuck the adventure. I made a safe trip and by the time our adventrist Lieutenant was shivering and shaking as though he had a chill. He got on the still block that stood handy and was putting on his close. He was just pulling on the last boot when our watch wheeled hisstreed and says look out. I looked round as the feds was in full gallop with in one hundred yds of us. Before we could get turned there foremost platoon wheld into line. By the time we were fifty yds from that spot they fired too many platoons at us. The Lieutenants mare being by the still, he made his escape leaving only a dirk knife on the stil. The Lieutenant, having a quantity of government money, of course was weary from capsizing of the canoe, he gave me his pocket book as he was wet and had him self to dry and told me to dry the money and keep it until he called for it. I had not bin acquainted with him only a few days.

Wer staid in this vicinity watching the Feds until the next day when we had some small adventures. My self and my too brothers was fired on by some pickets. About the first of April we was ordered to Missouria by the way of Pine Bluff where we crost the Arkansas river. We proceeded up the river to Litle Rock and campt at our old camp ground Camp Shipland. From here we proceeded north to the state of missouria traveling night and day part of the time. After leaving Spring River where we rested some days at Paterson, Missouria, we captured som feds, one proved to be a cosen of one Captain Stone in our regt. They were parold.

Then from thence to Bloomfield and to White Water where Colonel Carters bodygard surprised a company of federals on picket and killed 3 or 4 and tuck as many prisoners. Thence to Cape Jeredoe on the Missippi River where we rrived about the 8 or 9 of May, if I mistake not, I kept no dairy from Jan to the 31 of May. Shelby atacted the feds at ntyhis place and gave them a close fite until the feds reinforced and drove us back. Our regt was not brought into action hear. Rote hear my horse gave out as we had made a force march for some days before we reacht this place. The morning of the attract we had run our horses for several miles in which time brother Jameses horse, as we went down a long slant, lost his balance and fell headlong to the ground hurting my brother som, not bad though.

From Cape Jeredoe, the feds run us about 9 or 10 days fighting in the rear every day. While at the Cape one of our men was pit out as a spy of Pisket and he made good hid escape to the feds. This raid was made under Mormiduke, The feds pursued us closely as we was fixing and crossing the Sant Francis River. It was hear that I with many others starved 2 days and nights not having any ntyhings to eat from Wedsday noon till Friday noon. Hear we made camp and keep the fedsin check until our troops all crost but a small portion of us, then about 10 oclock on Frida we made a rush for the river snd had just barley time to swim our horses across the river and cary our saddles across on a rude pole pontoon bridge that had bin made for that purpose. When the feds was clost at our wheels we march some too miles from the river after cutting our bridge loos and stopt to have some refreshments if we could find them which we did. While hear the feds got rang by us firing of our guns and they shelled us pretty clostly. They killed one horse in our regt. He was shot while hid rider wa on him.

We marcht from hear in peace down Crowlseys Ridge on the east side of White River to Talor Creek where we campt for some time. Herar our command fought the feds. One of our lieutenants was shot through the body but not fataly and allso Lieutenant Triplet of whom I have allreddy spoken was fatally wonded. I was not permitted to see him after the fight. I went to Elmors on the 31 of May and left June the 11th.

From hear we followed west of Desarc I was taken sick and was accompanied by my brothers and B, Johnston. I and Dave stopt at one house while James and Johnston each stopt at a different house. While stopt brother Dave got sick and I had to wait on him. We stopt here on the 14th of June and left on the 21st.

We march to Pine Bluff and crost Arkansas River thence sown Bayou Bertholemew where we found our command in Louisannia, arriving on the 4 of Julye, 1863, after a long and weresom journey for a sick man.... Here we campt round in the swamp until late in August. At than time I, with about 20 others, was sent over on the Missippi River on a scout. After being out some days and making no discovery we turnd to march for our command. One day before we got to where we left our command we run in to federals and they had us cut off from our command. For too days we had to lay in the swamp sometime pressing us a guide and sometime without one. We made our appearance to our anxious comrads.

From hear we went to Camp Prisquiah in Claborn Parish La. courier Line at Mr. Morlands on the 30th of Sept and was relived November the 8th. While hear my company was ordered to Texas. I went from hear to Marshall Texas to my company, from hear to Athens where we was disbanded December the 21st and I made my way home....landed Dec the 22nd.

I left Jan the 3rd 1864. I landed at Crockett Jan 11th, as we (brother Dave and Joe Harden) was the first at the place of rendezvous, we reported to the postn commander. We was sent out on a scout to pick up conscripts and diserters. On one of our trips we pict up a suspicious man and while guarding him the first night, prisoner had an occasion to go out many times. Harding, being on guard thought the man true to come back, did not follow him out. The man left and did not come back. Harding dawoke us and told of his escape. I at once saw the danger of his stealing some of our horses as the one that he had been riding was very poor as well as small. I told the boys we had better guard the lot. He left his horse, saddle, saddle bags with some things in them, also one mexican spur which I took control of and have it to this day. The horse was turned over to the commander at Crockett.

Then on the 21 of Jan (it seamed that the 21 was a lucky day with me), I got a furlough for 60 days. I landed home on the 24th. While at home about the 8th of Feb. at the town of Dallas I saw and undoubtedly fell in love with my wife. I went to see her on the 14th of Feb, and again on the 21. At that time we was promist to be married and was married on the 28th of Feb, 1864 by one Sqyire James Clements of Scyene.

I left home Aprile the 13th, I came up with he company Aporile the 25th just after the Battle mon Mansfield and Pleasant Hill. I found our command above Alexandre on the Red River in La. I started home the 8th, landed May 14th. I left home May the 21st, I landed June the 2nd. My self and too brothers stopt sick at Captain Haleys in La.

August the 8th and left the 28th and stopt at Williams the 3rd of Sept. the 16th on Bayou Bartholomew. Brother Jim caught up with us here. My self and brother Jim stopt at Taylors on the Bayouas our command march off I was very sick. Then Jim tuck the fever and I had to wait on him. We stopt hear Oct 5th and left on Nov the 5th, caught up with our command about Nov, 10th or 12th at Walnut Hill in Arkansas. From hear our command march to Shrievport and hear I was keep so long that I giv my horse for a furlow and one hundred dollars in confed money. I only got $30 dollars down, the rest I have not got yett. I started the 11th of December in company with Andy Ealam. We landed the 17 or 18th. I never returned to command as I never got stout enough. The war ended about Aprile 1865.

I moved to Slap Foot that summer, built on Brother Dave's land and lived until Aprile '67. We bought a piece of land near by and made a farm on it. Our oldest child was born Feb 16, 66 and in 1867 we had another heir born—Jan the18th and she died Sept the 13th, 1869 I sold out here in Sept 1869 and bought a place on North Mesquite and here we had another heir born Nov. 28th '69. I sold out hear in the fall of 71 and bought in Scene. Hear November the 18th,.'71 we had another heir born. In the fall of '72 we moved on Mothers Place and in the fall of 73 I built and moved here Jan 11th, 74. Hear we had another heir born May 20, '74 and another girl bornd March 13th, 1876.

THE END

The above statement was added to his journal, so I left it as written. Helen tried to transcribe the journal as he wrote it, and I left it as she interpreted it. I am sure that a lot of it was difficult to read since over a hundred years had passed.

IV.

WHAT WAS THE LAST BATTLE
OF THE CIVIL WAR?

13

Distant friends are soon forgotten
Time soon washes their trails away
But I wish to be remembered
No matter where I stray

The final battle of the Civil War was fought at Palmito Ranch, Texas. The Confederate forces were led by Colonel John S. "Rip" Ford. The Union forces were led by Colonel H. Barrett.[16]

It was a hard-fought battle on May 12 and 13, 1865. Col. Theodore H. Barrett knew that Robert E. Lee had surrendered to Ulysses S. Grant several days before. Even though there was a gentleman's agreement to end the war, Barrett decided that several hundred of his best troops could destroy a large Confederate Camp. Barrett dispatched 250 men from the 62nd U.S. Colored Infantry and 50 men from the 2nd Texas Cavalry Regiment to the mainland. On May 11, he left with the intention of attacking the Confederate forces camped at the White and Palmito Ranches near Brownsville, Texas.

They arrived at the White ranch to find the Confederate army had vacated the ranch.

Col. Ford had the advantage with six cannon guns that were deadly against the Union Troops.

There were a total of at least 900 men and a total of 123 casualties. The Union suffered 117, and the Confederates suffered six.

The Confederate forces almost captured the Union Army, but the 62nd Cavalry was able to escape through a route left open.

Ford chased Barrett's men almost seven miles before calling off the pursuit. This ended the Battle of Palmito Ranch.

There are several accounts of this battle and the total number of troops involved. The total number of killed and wounded is also in dispute. What is not in dispute is the fact that this was the final battle of the Civil War.

There were several of the 62nd Colored Regiment captured at the Battle of Palmito Ranch. They were led to believe that if they were captured, they would either be shot or returned to slavery. Neither happened, and they were paroled and permitted to leave with the white prisoners of war. [17]

The last soldier killed in the Civil War was John W. William, who died at the Battle of Palmito Ranch.[18]

GRANDMOTHER'S POETRY

56

When we are old we will smile and say
We had no care in childhood day
But we will be wrong twill not be true
I had this one care I care for you

S ometimes in writing poetry, you make up a word because it just
sounds good and fits. In poem number 65 above, my grand-
mother used the word "twill." I liked it, but wondered if it was
a good word. After looking it up, I could not find a definition in
Webster's where it was used the way she did. *Webster's* used it to
describe a type of weave in fabric.[19] There was a British poet, C. T.
Studd (1860-1931), who used it in a famous religious poem titled
Only One Life. The lines where he used the word are as follows:

Only one life, twill soon be past,
Only what's done for Christ will last[20]

I have not been able to find a good date for that particular poem, and wonder who used it first, my grandmother or Studd? If the poem was published before she wrote this, then she could have read it and used the word. Or, as most poets do, maybe she just made it up.

Here are a few more of my grandmother's poems that I particularly enjoyed:

16

You are pretty you are witty
You are single what a pity
When you get old and cannot see
Put on your specs and think of me

25

When on this page in future years
You cast your smiles perhaps your tears
Lest thoughts of me engage your hearts
And remember the one that this page wrote

29

When the golden sun is sitting
And your heart from care is full
While are a thousand things you are thinking
Will you sometimes think of me

70

Meet me early
Meet me late
Meet me at
The golden Gate

73

Flowers may wither
Roses may die
You may forget
But never will I

86

As sure as the grapes
Grow on the vine
I'll be yours
If you'll be mine

87

Love is sweet
Love is bitter
Love your girl
And then can't get her

2

Is it vain in life's wide see
To ask you to remember me
Undoubtedly it is my lot
Just to be loved by him
And then be forgot

10

The rose is red the stem is green
The time has bin that we have seen
And yet I hope the time has come
When you and I will be as one

11

A mighty pain to love it is
And tis a pain that join to me
But of all the greatest pain
It is to love and love in vain

12

As sure as comes your wedding day
A broom to you I'll send
In sunshine rise the brushy joint
In storm the other end

Here is one of my poems giving thought to hers. I write a type of free verse that does not always rhyme, but tells a story my way.

I can tell she had a sense of humor
and gave her thoughts freely.
I almost changed the spelling of some of her words
Then old Webster said nope, she used it correctly.

THE LIFE AND TIMES OF H. B. COX

41

Some little token of regard
You wish from me today
But as time is pressing hard
I will but write my name

In his journal, H. B. related a story about witnessing the legal hanging of a woman in 1851. She was convicted of killing a man with an axe. He wrote that, "They stood her on her coffin and drove the wagon out from under her." Times were tough back then.

There are at least two cemeteries of importance where some of my family members are buried. The Glover Cemetery in East Dallas County, located at 6600 Military Parkway, is one of them. There are over 70 burials in this cemetery. The first burial was a little five-year-old girl, Sarah Jane Beeman. Many of Margaret Beeman-Bryan's family are buried here. Margaret was John Neely Bryan's wife. He is given credit as being the founder of Dallas, Texas.[21] Margaret was also a cousin of H. B. Cox. Margaret is buried in the Riverside Cemetery in Wichita Falls, Texas. She died September 6, 1919, at the age of 93.

The other cemetery of importance for my family is the Rylie Cemetery located in Rylie, Texas, where H. B. was buried.

The first burial in the Rylie cemetery, though, was Reddon Allumbaugh. My father, grandfather, and grandmother, May Belle Cox Allumbaugh, are buried there along with other relatives.

H. B. served as the postmaster of Rylie Prairie, Dallas County, Texas. He was instrumental in the layout of the streets and lots in Rylie Prairie, Texas. According to a letter from the postmaster in Dallas, he was probably the one who shortened the name from Rylie Prairie to just Rylie, Texas.

He also served as the railroad agent. The primary duties of a railroad agent are to assist passengers with ticketing and reservations and to offer information about routes, schedules, and fares. There are other duties as well, including the cleanliness of the depot and to ensure the safety of all passengers. The railroad agent, by and large, is the official representative of the railroad company.

During all this time, he was also a reporter for the *Mesquiter* newspaper. He became a correspondent for the paper soon after it was established in 1882 by the late R. S. Kimbrough, and he kept that position until about a year before he passed away. He was forced to give it up due to his failing eyesight. He was also a lay minister and farmer in his time. He and his first wife, Luthary Moore Cox, were among the founding members of the Rylie Christian Church. On Sunday, June 21, 2009, they held their 125th birthday celebration. The church held services until 2013.

The building was then sold and is now the A+ Academy Early Education Center.

I attended several services at the church, and at the time, did not realize the true history of my grandmother, the church, and the City of Dallas.

VII.

THE FIRST PERSON BORN IN DALLAS

1

I love but thee I love but thee with a
Love that will not die
Till the stars grow cold and the
Moon is old and the leaves of the
Judgement book unfold

John Neely Bryan married Margaret Beeman, a close cousin of H. B.'s. John is given the distinction of founding Dallas, Texas.[22] Bryan was born in 1810 and died in 1877. In November 1841, he arrived and settled on the banks of the Trinity River. In 1892, there was a book written that stated his son, John Jr., was the first white male born in Dallas in the year 1844, but this is incorrect.

In 1844, the town was surveyed and laid out, and Dallas County was formed in 1846. On February 2, 1856, the Texas Legislature granted Dallas a town charter. [23]

As with a lot of history, there are conflicting reports that John Jr. had a sibling born before him, on August 26, 1944, who did not live very long after birth. This child's name was Coffee Holland Bryan, and he is buried in the Beeman Cemetery located on the west bank of White Rock Creek. Despite reports otherwise, Coffee was, in fact, the true firstborn of John Neely Bryan and Margaret Beeman, and therefore the firstborn in Dallas.

* * *

The following is a word-for-word quote by Hartwell Bolin Cox that should lay to rest the true history about the first person born in Dallas. It was dated August 1, 1914, and published in the *Dallas Times Herald on* August 2, 1914.

Mesquite, Texas, August 1, 1914
I see William Glover claims to be the oldest settler in Dallas county. I knew his mother was a widow Stockton before she and his father were married. She lived north of Dallas in 1844 and two brothers and myself went to her house one day when we were running away from the Indians. We were living near where the convent now stands. When we got there she had two or three guns standing in the corner of her house, but the Indians never came. This was in 1844 before Glover was born. I have a cousin Scott Beeman, who lives in or near Dallas. He came here in April 1842. There is not another person living in Dallas who came in 1842. He has a sister living in Clay County who came here in 1842. She is the widow of the founder of Dallas, John Neely Bryan who should have a monument built in

Dallas to his memory. It is a shame that it has not already been built. Back to my subject. James N. Cochran was born June 1846 in Dallas. Brian was born in Dallas February 9, 1846. He had one brother born before him. His name was Coffee Brian. He died while young.

My brother G.W. Cox had a daughter born in his county August 9, 1845. The first legislature of this state on 30 March 1846, passed an act creating the county of Dallas. Glover claims he was born on 31 July 1846 ten days after the county was created. He missed his guess by about 110 days. I'll have lived in Dallas county since the spring of 1844 except while in the late war between the states, my home was here while I was in the war. I am not envying Glover for his claims, but the record kept straight for he and I are good friends, I could fill many pages telling of our early life in Dallas County. Yours Truly, H. B. Cox, Mesquite, Texas, route number four.

It is important to note that at the time of the account, of going to the widow's home, H. B. would have only been four years old. His brothers were older, and they could have taken him with them at the time of the incident. This is also the same year that they arrived in the area.

VIII.

MORE POEMS WRITTEN BY MAY BELLE COX

31

Round is the ring
That has no end
So is my love to you
My friend

32

The sea is wide
The water is deep
And in you arms
I hope to sleep

33

Some loves many
Some loves few
Remember me
And I will you

34

Remember dear
Remember true
Remember me
And I will you

35

Some loves one
Some loves too
I love one
And that is you

37

Remember love remember true
Remember me and I will you
And if the grave should be my bed
Remember me when I am dead

44

I think of thee all day
I dream of thee at night
My heart has no respite
From pain whilst thou art away

49

These few lines to you is tender
By a friend sincere and true
Hoping to be remembered
When I am far away from you

56

Come all young men
With rambling minds
And listen to my
Mournful song

59

I had a heart and it was true
It has gone from me and followed you
So you have too
And I have none

61

Here's a sigh to those that love me
Here's a smile to those that hate
And whatever sky's above me
Here's a heart for every fate

62

Forget me not till death shall close
My eyelids in them last repose
And summer breezes gently blow
The green grass ore my lonely grave

69

Always remember
And never forget
The blue eyed girl
Who loves you yet

75

Birds have flowers
Flowers have dew
I love but one
That one is you

79

The evening star
And the morning dew
Is not to be compared
With a kiss from you

80

If were a husband you should have
And he this book should see
Tell him of your thoughtful days
And kiss him once for me

81

I wish the health
I wish the wealth
I wish the heaven after death
How can I wish the more

There were times when she may have misspelled a word. I tried to leave them as she wrote them. Because of the age of the Almanac, a few words were hard to make out, as they were written in pencil, so I did not try to put those poems in this book. Sometimes, one word can change the whole meaning of a poem. The last poem in the book was this next one.

89

When times don't go to suit you
And the world seems upside down
Want not your time for fretting
But drive away the frown

IX.

H. B.'S OUTLAW HISTORY

50

Perhaps at some time we must part
And it is with an earnest heart
That I ask thee while in glee
Or in sorrow remember me

I am not sure how my great-grandfather came to know Cole Younger, but he proved to be an influential person in my great-grandfather's life. It could have been while Cole's brother, Jim, was a sheriff in Dallas County, or due to his being a neighbor of Myra Shirley. He apparently thought enough of her that he named my grandmother after her.

To give you some background, Cole Younger was born in 1844. Cole was born into a family of fourteen children. They were raised on the family farm near Lee's Summit, Missouri. Four of the boys would go out to be outlaws. They were Cole (1844-1916), Jim (1851-1902), John (1851-1874), and Bob (1853-1889).

Jim Younger was the Dallas sheriff in 1870 and 1871. He later joined up with his brothers Cole, John, and Bob Younger. They then joined up with Jesse James and his gang. They went on a bloody crime spree all across the South.

H. B.'s first wife, Louthary Ann Moore, was my grandmother's mother. She had six brothers and sisters. Myra Maybelle Shirley was a neighbor and served as the midwife at the birth of her sister, Mary Lou Cox. At the time, Myra Maybelle Shirley lived with her parents in Scyene, Texas, a small town near H. B's home in Rylie Prairie, Texas.

Myra Maybelle Shirley would later become known as "Belle Starr the Bandit Queen."

Belle Starr

Belle Starr was born as Myra Maybelle Shirley on February 5, 1848, near Carthage, Missouri. Her father, John R. Shirley, and her mother, twenty years younger than her husband, were Elizabeth Hatfield Shirley, who was related to the Hatfield family of the Hatfield-McCoy feud. [24]

She attended the Carthage Female Academy, where she excelled in her studies and learned several languages.[25] She also became an accomplished pianist. After her brother, Ben Shirley, was shot and killed by Union Troops, her dad was heartbroken.[26] He sold his business and property and moved to Texas, traveling in a Conestoga wagon. Myra lived through most of the 1870s near Dallas, Texas. The tragic events of the Civil War helped mold Myra into the outlaw that she would become. She met up with Cole Younger and Jesse James, which further hardened her to the outlaw way of life.[27]

In 1866, at the age of 20, she entered into a common law marriage to Jim Reed. He supposedly ran with Jesse James and was shot and killed eight years later. In 1880, Belle married Bruce Younger, who disappeared only three weeks into the marriage. His body was later discovered in a cave in New Mexico. She married a third time to Sam Starr, a Cherokee Indian who was shot and killed during a gunfight on December 18, 1887.[28]

Earlier in 1883, Sam and Belle were arrested by U.S. Marshal Bass Reeves, a famous black Marshall, and taken before Judge Issac Parker, known as the hanging Judge, of Fort Smith, Arkansas. They were sentenced to nine months in a federal prison for horse theft.[29]

In December of 1816, while celebrating at a Christmas dance, Sam Starr was shot and killed during a gunfight with a cousin by the name of Richard West. They both died of their gunshot wounds. Belle married for the fourth time to Jim July, a Creek Indian. After two years of marriage, on February 3, 1889, she was shot and killed. She had been shot in the back, face, and head from a shotgun blast. Her daughter Pearl heard the shot from her cabin, and Belle died in her arms.[30]

While it was never proven who shot and killed Belle, her own son was a suspect. She was buried in her front yard near Younger's Bend, Oklahoma.

Her tombstone quoted a popular poem at the time:
Shed not for her the bitter tear

Nor give the heart to vain regret
Tis but the casket that lies here
The gem that fills it sparkles yet

Her husband, Jim July, was shot and killed a year later on January 26, 1890, in a gunfight with Deputy Marshals Bob Hutchins and Bob Trainer, and is buried in Fort Smith, Arkansas.[31]

* * *

More About Cole Younger

As I said before, Cole Younger was an influential person in my great-grandfather's life.

When the Jayhawkers, a militant group associated with the free state cause during the American Civil War, raided the Youngers' farm and killed their dad in 1862, Cole and Jim joined and rode with Quantrill's raiders. (The term "Jayhawker" was later used to describe Union Troops led by abolitionists from Kansas.[32] After the war, it became synonymous with anyone living in the Kansas territory.)

In 1863, Quantrill's raiders went into Lawrence, Kansas, with a vengeance not often seen. They killed between 160 and 190 men and boys. Younger later said that it was a brutal attack but admitted, "There was nothing in my life so thrilling as my part in the raid on Lawrence."[33]

Cole and his brothers were very bitter towards the Kansas Militia because of the murder of his father, the assault of his sister, and the mistreatment of their mother. One of the reasons given for robbing northern banks was to get back at the feds for killing their father.

The northern occupation of Missouri made it difficult for anyone who fought on the side of the Confederacy to live there. They had a lot of animosity towards the people in the reconstruction of Missouri. All of this helped to mold Cole and his brothers into the outlaw way of life.

Following the Civil War, the Younger Brothers began robbing banks and trains when they joined up with Jesse and Frank James. In 1874, John Younger was killed during a bank robbery attempt at Northfield, Minnesota. It became known as the Northfield Raid, one of the bloodiest bank robberies in Minnesota. The James-Younger gang was accused of a lot of crimes they did not commit. Some reports say that Cole only participated in eight bank robberies, and with the exception of Northfield, all the robberies were well-planned, and no one was killed. Other reports state that the James/Younger gang went on to commit as many as 12 bank robberies, five train robberies, five stagecoach robberies, and also stole the gate cashbox of the Kansas City Exposition.[34]

No matter their outlaw ways, they believed in the finest horseflesh that they could find. Jesse himself owned a racehorse named "JIM MALONE," which reportedly won $5,000 in 26 starts in 1880 and 1881. Jessie also owned another racehorse, "SKYROCKET," that raced at Monmouth Park in 1875-76. They also frequented many resorts such as Monegaw Springs in St. Clair County, Missouri, and Hot Springs, Arkansas. For most of their outlaw days, there were no pictures of them, and they could travel as they wanted without being recognized.

They became well known back east and dime store novels were being written about their exploits. Most of the novels had nothing to do with who they really were but were good, fun reading.

During the years when they were robbing banks, Cole spent a lot of time in Texas. He spent some time with Myra Maybelle Shirley, and she claimed her first child was his. He always denied it, but I suspect that she knew to whom her first baby belonged.

In 1876, several of the James-Younger gang were wounded or killed in the same town as their earlier robbery at Northfield, Minnesota. Frank and Jesse escaped, three members of their gang were killed, and after a two-week pursuit, the Younger Brothers were captured. Cole had been wounded eleven times, Jim five times, and Bob four times. Bob died in prison of tuberculosis. Jim committed suicide after being released from prison.

I have not found a direct link to Jesse James and my great-grand-dad, but Jesse did spend a lot of time in Texas and in close proximity to Myra Belle Shirley. He and Cole were very close friends, and it stands to reason that they crossed paths at times.

Jesse James married his first cousin, Zerelda Mimms, who was named after Jesse's own mother. They had two children together, Jesse E. James and Mary (James) Barr.

On April 3,1882, at the age of 34, Jesse James was shot and killed by a gang member, Robert Ford, a new recruit to the gang.[35] He hoped to collect the reward on Jesse's head. He had been promised amnesty for his previous crimes.

John Younger was killed in a shootout by a Pinkerton agent on March 17,1874.

Alexander Franklin James, the older brother of Jesse James, was born January 10, 1843, and died February 18, 1915, in Kearney, Missouri.

Cole made the statement that if he and his brothers wanted to, they could have escaped the jail they were being held in when they were first arrested. He had a lot of regrets about the things he had done and now wanted his story told. He and his brothers took the punishment as meted out by the court of Minnesota.

Cole survived his wounds and, after 19 years in prison, retired to the Younger farm at Lee's Summit. Cole got out of prison in 1901 and boarded the train at Saint Paul, knowing that to honor his pardon, he would never return to Minnesota. In 1903, he was granted a full pardon.

While Cole was in prison, the outside world was changing, and he saw his first trolley car, and it is said that he was transfixed by the sight.

He wrote a life history of his brothers and himself, putting them in a sympathetic light. This really couldn't be further from the truth. No matter what excuse he used for leading the life he had led, he was still a bloodthirsty killer. He left a trail of blood all across parts of the Kansas territory. Many parts of the northern states felt his vengeance.

For a short time, he joined with Frank James and went on the lecture circuit, preaching about the evils of the outlaw way of life. They were billed as "The Great Cole Younger and Frank James Historical Wild West Show." One of their performances was on September 2, 1903, near Boonville, Missouri.

Others were influenced by the life that they had led, and one of them became known as Billy the Kid, who went on to lead an outlaw life of his own.

Between Minnesota and Missouri, Cole had decided that he wanted people to know him and how he came to be where he was. During his incarceration, he became a minister.

After his release, he visited with my great-grandfather in Rylie, Texas. Cole gave a sermon at H. B.'s church, and after the service, had dinner at his home. It was said that after dinner, Cole went out to H. B.'s backyard and dug something up. This may or may not be true, but I suppose it is very possible that that was the real reason he returned to Texas. It was believed that what he dug up was money. Paper money, after all those years, would not have been in very good shape.

Thomas Coleman Younger was born on January 15, 1844, in Jackson County, Missouri, and died in 1916, of natural causes, at his home in Lee's Summit, Missouri. He is buried at the Lee's Summit Historical Cemetery next to his parents and siblings.

PICTURES

Original Pocket Almanac

2014 Corvette Stingray

2002 Fat Boy Harley Davidson

Jerry Coker and Charles at the Dallas Naval Air Station in 1963.

In 1953, Jerry Silvers, owner of the Uptown and Wings Theater, cutting a watermelon on stage. The theatre held Saturday morning Matinees and put on shows for the kids of Grand Prairie, TX. Charles McKenzie, pictured as the clown.

The Flying Red Horse on top of the Mobile Building,
circa 1947. Photo taken from the Mercantile Bank Building.

Frank Alumbaugh working on the Mercantile Bank Tower, 1947.

Construction of the Mercantile Bank Building spire, 1947.

1933, Fairy Viola Fort behind the counter, first waitress from the left with a white flower in her hair. W. T. Grants, downtown Dallas, TX

Cullum and Boren, a semiprofessional baseball team, 1920s. Frank Allumbaugh is located in the second row, positioned in the center.

All the officials for the 1926 Texas State Fair. They are
standing in the old grandstand where horse races were held.
Steven Strickland Allumbagh, 6th from the right, second
row. He was the official Blacksmith for several years.

May Belle and Family, 1910.

H. B. Cox Family Reunion 1899.

H. B. Cox and Family.

May Belle Cox (middle), 1882.

1883, Appointment to Postmaster of Ryle, TX
Timothy O. Howe, lawyer, District Judge, Senator, Justice of the
Wisconsin Supreme Court, and Wisconsin pioneer. While in the
Senate, President Ulysses S. Grant offered him the position of Chief
Justice of the Supreme Court. He declined the offer for fear that
a Democrat would follow him in his position as Senator. He was
appointed Postmaster General by President Chester A. Arthur in 1881.
He signed this Postmaster appointment on March 6, 1883, appointing
H. B. Cox was the first Postmaster of Rylie, Texas. After returning
home, he died on March 25, only 19 days after signing the letter. This
would have been one of his last official duties as Postmaster General.

1881, A. M. Cochran, Postmaster of Dallas, explaining
how to pick the name for the post office of Ryle, TX.

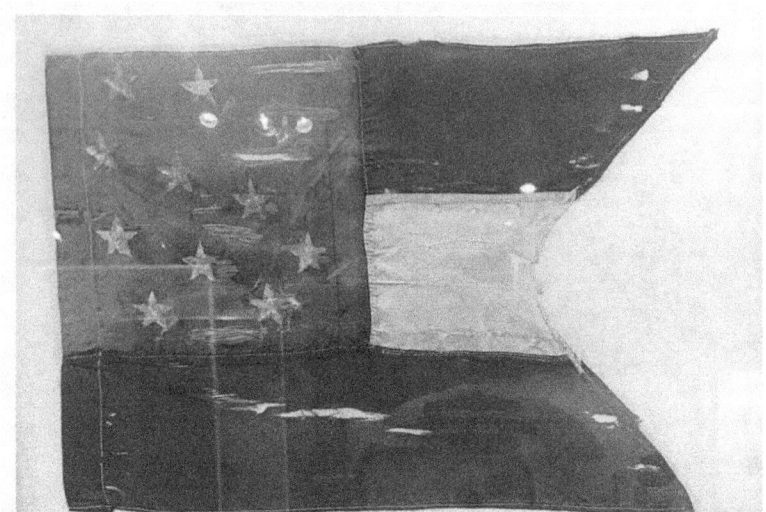

20th Texas Battle Flag, Dallas, TX.

Company B, 19th Texas Cavalry
Attached to Parson's Brigade formed in Dallas 1862 by
Nathanial M. Buford. Disbanded in Marshall, Texas
in 1865. Served under Captain Allen Beard.

ORIGIN OF THE ALLUMBAUGH FAMILY NAME

51

When the name I write here is dim with age
And the leaves of your album are yellow
Still think of me kindly and do not forget
That wherever I am I remember you yet

In 1961, Donna Alumbaugh began recording and researching the history of the Allumbaugh/Alumbaugh family. She started by asking known family members for their knowledge about the Allumbaugh/Alumbaugh family. In 2001, she printed the second family history with 1,450 pages (including the index). Every family member can now trace their history back to Peter Allumbaugh and his children, from whom they descend. Her research included professors in Germany, helping to fill in some of the possible history of the Allumbaugh/Alumbaugh family. Following are several quotes from her book—some are hers, and some are mine. The list of family names and birth dates is also taken from her book. We owe a debt of gratitude to Donna and her husband, Max, for preserving this record. I also provided a history of my immediate family, which is included in the book.

In the year of our LORD 1740, there was a boy born somewhere in Germany. There are some records, mostly handed down by word of mouth, that he was born in Baden-Baden, Germany.

Life was hard in those times, very, very hard. His parents decided to take him and all the family, numbering 14 in all, and travel to a strange new world. Some records handed down by word-of-mouth state different numbers for the family.

It is believed that they traveled to Holland and boarded a boat in or around 1754, to this new land. They could have boarded the ship in Rotterdam, Holland. At that time in Rotterdam, when boarding a vessel, only the head of household was required to record his name. Unfortunately, the records for this period have been lost.

The name in Germany could have been spelled Allenbach, and in German, it is clearly pronounced Allumbaugh.

During this trip, cholera broke out on the ship, and all of his brothers and sisters and his parents died and were buried at sea.

At the young age of 14 and unable to read or write, he found himself in the New World, alone with no family for support. There were two families on the ship that also lost two or three of their children, and they took Peter into their family and raised him.

The exact place that they embarked to start their life in this New World has been lost to history, but it is believed that they may have landed near old Jamestown, Virginia. It is quite possible that his boat embarked in the Chesapeake Bay area near old

Jamestown, and Peter traveled up the York River in another boat to King William's County, Virginia.

In his Revolutionary War pension application, he stated he lived in King William County, so there is some record to substantiate this theory.

To reach King William County, he would have traveled up the York River to the present site of West Point. At that time, West Point was a tobacco plantation, and they would have been in need of skilled workers.

Some of Peter's children, numbering eleven in all, spelled their name in a few different ways.

His firstborn was John Allumbaugh, born about 1770.

Then came:

- Elizabeth Allumbaugh "Betsey," born about 1779
- Nancy Allumbaugh born about 1783/84
- Peter Allumbaugh/Alumbaugh
- Barbara Allumbaugh
- Garrett Allumbaugh was born April 1, 1789. (My direct descendant)
- Mary Allumbaugh/Alumbaugh "Polly," about 1794
- Margaret Allumbaugh was born about 1795
- Katie Allumbaugh was born about 1795
- Christina Allumbaugh was born about 1797
- _____ Allumbaugh (Daughter), date of birth unknown

The name of Allumbaugh has also been spelled as: Alenbaugh, Allenbough, Elembaugh & Ellumbaugh. All are descendants of the "original" Peter Allumbaugh.

During the decade of 1765 to 1774, many Germans learned a trade and were known for their crafts. Peter learned to be a blacksmith and was employed as a cooper. A cooper is a craftsman who made and repaired barrels and casks. It was a very important way to store food stuff and gunpowder. He possibly made barrels to transport supplies up the nearby New and Kanawha rivers in West Virginia.

Many of Peter's descendants were called jack-of-all-trades, and this ability probably came from Peter. My own grandfather was a blacksmith.

THE JOHN NEELY BRYAN CABIN
AND BUCKNER ORPHANS HOME

64

Think of me in the hour of leisure
Think of me in the hour of care
Think of me in the hour of pleasure
Spare me one thought in the hour of prayer

As long as I can remember, there has been a small cabin on the courthouse lawn in Dallas that was supposed to be the original cabin that John Neely Bryan, the founder of Dallas, owned. Neither it nor the two that have followed was actually his cabin, however.

I can remember my dad and some of his brothers taking my grandmother to Dallas to confirm if the first one on the courthouse lawn was actually his cabin. She remembered seeing the cabin. Her dad, H. B. Cox, had spent the night in the cabin, and it is possible that over the years he had more than one cabin in the area, but we know that the one on the lawn in Dallas was not the one she remembered. (I have since read that it was a replica of his cabin, and that is probably more accurate.)

The original cabin was loaned to and displayed in 1926 at the Texas State Fair. After the fair, the cabin was being stored on the grounds of the Buckner Orphans Home in Dallas, Texas. A fire broke out, and it was burned, and a few of the logs went missing.

Robert Cook Buckner, a Baptist pastor from Tennessee, convinced the Baptist Deacons Convention in 1877 to pass a resolution to start an orphan's home as soon as $2,000 had been raised.

Buckner wrote a charter and filed it with the state of Texas on April 9, 1879. The following December, it was opened in a rented house with three children. In 1880, Buckner purchased a forty-four-acre tract of land for 17 dollars an acre. Six children moved to the new home in 1881. By the turn of the century, there were almost 500 children being cared for.

FAMILY TIES TO THE TEXAS STATE FAIR

72

May your life be always happy
May your smiles be always gay
Like the lilies of the valley
When they bloom in lovely May

I have a picture of the officials for the 1926 State Fair standing in the old grandstand. Steven Strickland Allumbaugh, my grandfather, is standing in the center, as he was the official blacksmith for the fair.

May Belle Cox married my grandfather, Steven Strickland Allumbaugh, in December 1895. She was 22 years old, and they went on to have 11 children. It seems strange today for someone to have so many children, but it was not unusual back then. She was also a very small, petite woman. She had to be strong mentally and physically to run the household the way she did. I am sure I am not the only one to wish I could go back and talk about those early years growing up in Texas.

I hope that anyone reading this book will do just that. If you have grandparents still living, please ask them about their early years and what it was like growing up. You may be surprised by some of the things they did and the things they remember.

While she took care of the homestead, Steve worked as a farmer, ran a dairy farm, and had a blacksmith shop in the back of the property where several of my cousins and I would play all summer long. This was in the late 40s and early 50s, and my dad and his brothers finally tore it down because they were afraid some of us would get hurt.

One day, my dad and I were driving down Master Drive in his '39 Plymouth, and he was pointing out some memories from his childhood. I remember him saying that a saloon used to stand on a certain spot as we passed. He also mentioned that there was a farmhouse that stood on a hill near Mesquite, so they could see the Indians as they approached the farmhouse.

My father was born in 1899 and saw a lot of changes during his time. He told me about the first radio he ever heard. It had a speaker of some type, and everyone would sit around listening to their favorite sport. Boxing was very big, and of course, baseball was also very popular. They would sit around talking, and watch the traffic go by, and they would remark how cars would "zip by" at 10 or 15 miles per hour. They nicknamed that intersection Zip City. I believe there was an auto shop where all this took place. It may have been at the intersection of Lake June and Peachtree Road. I am sure someone will correct me if I am wrong about the location. I have not been able to verify this, but I do know the story was true about the area being called Zip City.

There was an elderly German couple who lived next to their service station and grocery store. We would visit them when we went back to my grandparents, and I would go out front to pump the gas into the glass container on top so we could buy gas for our car. With hindsight, they probably wished I would not do that. They never did stop me, though.

I can remember my dad saying that he helped Steve, as my granddad was called, clear land and turn the wood into charcoal so they could sell it to the neighbors. It seems that he was into anything that would put food on the table.

I remember his corn fields where he grew sweet corn, popcorn, and other crops. He had a horse he called Big Red, that he used to plow his field. I remember seeing him plow that field. It would have been in the early to mid '40s.

He tried to teach me how to milk a cow, and my grandmother showed me how to wring a chicken's neck. I never did perfect either one.

They had very large gatherings of family and friends. I found an article from a paper that said on their 50th anniversary, there were about 500 people in attendance.

For several years, he was the official blacksmith for the State Fair of Texas. I have a picture taken in 1926 with him standing in the old grandstands with all the officials of the fair for that year.

I remember my dad saying that he was one of the few who could make and shoe the Clydesdale horses. I do not know for sure if he shod the Budweiser Clydesdale horses because they only came into existence in 1933. I remember my dad saying that he did.

I do not know the exact years that he worked at the fair. It may have been about 11 or 12 years as I have some cookbooks from the fair that belonged to my grandmother for some of those years.

Several of my cousins and I would play in the old blacksmith shop, and one weekend, my dad and some of his brothers tore the building down, saying that it might fall down on us. I still have a few of the tools from the old farm. I had a toolbox with a lot of tools in it on my pickup, but one night, someone broke into it and stole the tools. I would still pay to get that back with no questions asked.

There was an aunt who lived next door, and I believe she ended up with the old buggy and turned it into a large flower pot in the corner of the yard. Jeez!

Some History of the State Fair of Texas

I had not planned on getting into the history of the Texas State Fair, but felt some of the early history was important, to put into context my grandfather's history at the fair, and my childhood memories of the fair.

The Texas State Fair actually began in Houston in 1870. The Mechanical and Bloodstock Association of Texas brought the first State Fair of Texas to Houston, but after several attempts at moving to different locations, they went bankrupt, and the state fair was closed in Houston.[36] The fair, as we now know it, in Dallas, was started up again as a private corporation. It became a popular and profitable venture. In 1904, a financial crisis caused the businessmen running the fair to sell it to the city of Dallas with the agreement that it would run for 24 days during the fall of the year.

In many ways, the state fair has been instrumental in helping to end segregation in Dallas. In the beginning, the fair was segregated. African Americans were only allowed to go to the fair one day during the entire run, "Negro Achievement Day." As such, the Dallas Negro Chamber of Commerce was under a lot of pressure to get the fair opened to all citizens. However, the white leaders of that day continued to deny that the fair was segregated. In the 1950s, Mayor R. L. Thornton agreed to desegregate some, but insisted that restrictions would still apply. Some restaurants and two rides that involve physical contact were still closed to the black population. In 1955, Juanita Craft (1902-1985) organized a protest against the policy of only admitting blacks on Negro Achievement Day. Juanita was the first black woman to vote in Dallas County and for twenty years was a Democratic Party precinct chair. In the 1950s, she helped open the University of Texas and North Texas State College to blacks.

In 1967, her youth group's efforts successfully and finally desegregated the State Fair of Texas. She stayed active in the civil rights movement for most of her life. Juanita was cremated and buried alongside other family members in Austin's Evergreen Memorial Cemetery.

In addition to Negro Achievement Day, the Texas State Fair has had other days designated as special days. These include: Colored Peoples Day, Ku Klux Klan Day, and, as late as the 1980s, a day was dedicated to the Confederacy.

As you can imagine, there have been many other controversies involving the State Fair and the African American community.

One such controversy was how officials for the fair bought up land for a parking lot at less than market value. All the property was owned by African Americans that lived in the area.

The State Fair was a big part of my growing up in Texas. There have been very few years that I have missed going. To this day, my wife of 65 years and I try to never miss going. Our first stop each year is the automobile building, and then on to enjoy Fletcher's corn dogs.

It does seem like the weather patterns have changed during the week of the fair. When I was young, it always seemed to be cold and rainy, but now it can be very warm. No doubt, there is a type of climate change from then to now.

DIFFERENT TIMES

65

When we are old we will smile and say
We had no care in childhood day
But we will be wrong twill not be true
I had this one care I care for you

I was born August 16, 1940, in St Paul's Hospital in Dallas, Texas.
I rode many of the early streetcars and spent a lot of time in
downtown Dallas. I remember the electric buses that took the
place of the streetcars. They were much quieter than the street-
cars and were used for several years. I also remember riding the
streetcars in Oak Cliff along Jefferson Blvd, a main thoroughfare
through Oak Cliff.

When the streetcar would get to the end of the line, the operator or conductor would have to go to the back of the streetcar and move the electrical connector so the streetcar could go the other direction.

My favorite place to eat was Dunton's Cafeteria on Elm Street, downtown near the theater district. My favorite thing to eat there was a turkey croquette. When I was five or six years old, we would ride the bus from Grand Prairie, Texas, to downtown Dallas. That was always a special day for me and remains a favorite memory of mine.

We would frequent the W. T. Grant's lunch counter. When my mother left west Texas she worked there and knew many of the women that still worked there, so she liked to visit them.

During those years, almost every small town had a train station, and most of them looked very similar to each other. There was a train station in town between Main Street and Jefferson Avenue. I remember riding the train to Sweetwater, Texas, where my mother's family lived. She had sisters that lived in Roscoe, and we enjoyed visiting with them.

The train rides were during the war, and I can actually remember that there were always soldiers or sailors on the train. When I was about three or four years old, my mother dressed me in a sailor suit. It seems strange to me now how much I can actually remember about my early years.

You'll Shoot Your Eye Out, Kid…

We all had guns from the time we were about 13 years old. I remember many times walking to a wooded area and shooting my .22 rifle. If a young person were seen walking down the street today with a gun, someone would call the police on them. Different times indeed… it never occurred to me that you could shoot someone else.

All through my high school years, we would have our guns on the gun rack on the back window of our truck in plain sight. We parked in the High School parking lot, and no one thought anything about it. No one ever had their vehicle broken into that I can remember.

I do not remember hearing about a shooting at a school anywhere. It just didn't happen.

Extended Family Memories

My grandmother on my mother's side lived in Sweetwater, Texas, and I would spend summers there. She lived with my Uncle Woodrow in his home, and I was never sure who took care of whom. It worked great for both of them. In WWII, he was a personal security guard for General Patton. His Army discharge papers show where he served. The only one I can recall from memory was the Battle of the Bulge. He never talked about it, and no one ever asked him, as far as I know. I only found out by reading his discharge papers after he passed away.

He taught me how to drive when I was about ten years old. He had a brand-new Pontiac, and I could not reach the pedals without sinking down in the seat, and then I could hardly see the windshield. Everyone told him I was going to kill both of us, but he would just laugh, and we would take off. I found out later that he let a cousin of mine do the same thing.

I had an aunt named Pearl that owned a home in Roscoe. She had a well with a windmill that pumped their bath water. The water was very hard and tasted terrible. When you took a bath, the soap wouldn't suds up, and hard water stains would be left in the bathtub. They also had a storm shelter, and we would stand near the entrance when storms were coming through the area in case of a tornado. I remember that she worked as a waitress at a local cafe in the middle of town. She would make chili in a large pan. That is the first time I remember eating a bowl of chili.

Early Years in Grand Prairie, Texas

I really do not know for sure how we ended up in Grand Prairie. I was only one year old when we moved there, and I don't know if my dad was working at the plant. My earliest recollection of his employment was when he worked at a neon sign company in Dallas. He had lived in St. Louis and was working on designing and doing layouts for signs there before moving back, and he and my mother married in 1938.

A friend of mine and I would ride the bus from Grand Prairie to Oak Cliff every Saturday morning to go swimming at the YMCA. I remember we swam in the nude because trunks were not allowed. It seems strange today, but then it was just the way it was. It was around 1953 or 1954.

I also remember when the Baghdad Supper Club burned. On April 19, 1953, Baghdad burned in what was called the most spectacular fire in western Dallas County. Millions of dollars in artwork and furnishings were destroyed. There were 45 paintings by the Hungarian artist Armand Grotz, one by Gainsborough, and a Van Dyke—all destroyed. The paintings alone at that time were valued at one million dollars. Of course, any one of them would bring a lot more than that today.

The supper club was built in 1929, and this was a great loss to Grand Prairie and West Dallas County when it burned down. The building was a Moorish-style, two-story building, clad in pinkish-gray stucco. The exterior had rounded spires and was distinctly oriental in all its features, and it sat on a 14-acre lot. The building was set back about 300 feet off what is now Highway 180. It had a parking lot for about 300 cars. The interior featured a stage and dance floor. It had dining rooms and lounging rooms. At that time, the dance floor was billed as the largest in the southwest. The main dining room could seat 450.

A day or two after the fire, several of us boys rummaged through the ruins while it was still smoldering. We found some large metal canisters with movie film in them that had somehow survived the fire. In the canisters was film with footage of all kinds of airplanes. The supper club was in line with the airstrip where planes built by North American Aviation took off and landed. Thousands of planes were built at that plant for the war effort. We kids started a rumor that the movies were taken by Japanese spies. The rumor floated around for several weeks.

TEMCO

My home was also under the flight pattern of the Texas Engineering Company (TEMCO), and dozens of planes took off day and night. We got used to the noise and could sleep right through all of it.

Two former executives started the Texas Engineering Company (TEMCO). In 1946, they employed about 2,500. Chance Vought then subleased the plant and moved 1,300 people and an amazing

28 million pounds of machinery 1,687 miles from Connecticut to Grand Prairie.

The company started as Fokker Aircraft, then General Aviation, and then North American Aviation. Robert McCullough was the factory manager in 1941. He then left to work for Convair in Nashville, Tennessee, and returned to North America in 1943.

TEMCO built planes for the war effort and turned out a record 728 planes in 30 days at the Grand Prairie, Texas, plant. At the height of production in 1944, they employed 38,500 people working three 8-hour shifts each day. They built about 20,000 planes during that time.

One of the planes they built was the P-51 Mustang. It was one of the fastest planes at 430 miles an hour and integral in helping to end the war. This was the plane made famous by the Tuskegee Airmen, a group of Black pilots. The war ended in December 1945. By that time, employment had dropped to about 15,000, and all employees lost their jobs.

There were several types of aircraft made at this location, both before and after World War II. These included: the T-6 Texan trainer, P-51 Mustang fighter, B-24 Bomber, F-86 Sabre, Jet fighter, and the F-35 Joint Fighter.

Later, the LTV Corporation built the Corsair and the Crusader. The Crusader became the most important fighter during the Vietnam era. This was the plane that John Glenn set a speed record from Los Angeles to New York in 3 hours and 23 minutes.

* * *

I remember the day the war ended. I was only five years old, but all the sirens in town were going off, and a Black lady that was babysitting next door came out on the back porch with a large pan and a wooden spoon. She was banging on the pan and repeating over and over that her baby was coming home. She was obviously glad the war was finally over. There were celebrations all over the country.

There was another airfield in Grand Prairie. That was known as the Curtis-Wright Airport of Fort Worth/Dallas. It actually came to Grand Prairie in 1929 and was operated as a flight training facility. They operated their flight school for about a year, then in 1940, the field became the Lou Foote Flying School. In 1942, the Navy took it over and established the Grand Prairie Naval Landing Field.

After the War, it was used as a glider port. It was known as the Texas Soaring Association. I remember going to a glider meet where gliders from all over the world came. In one contest, they would see how far one could travel without landing. At least one glider was from Germany, and I was shocked that an enemy airplane was in Grand Prairie. I do remember my dad laughing and saying something to the effect that the war was over. This was around 1947.

Dick Johnson was an aviation pioneer who helped bring the Soaring Association Meet to Grand Prairie. He was born in Alberta, Canada, in 1923. In 1939, at the age of 16, he bought and assembled a Bowlus Baby Albatross Kit and, with the help of his brother, built a wooden trailer. In 1940, he hauled it 3,000 miles from his home in California to Elmira, NY, for the national gliding championship. When he arrived, he had to get his pilot's license and a certification for his glider. After earning these, he then placed third in the contest.

In 1950, he brought an RJ-5 glider to Grand Prairie, where he won the first of 11 National Soaring Championships after making some improvements on his glider. He soared 535 miles, being the first glider pilot to soar more than 500 miles.[37] That record stood for 12 years. He went on to win several championships.

We would sometimes park and watch the gliders take off and land. There was a small plane used to lift the gliders to altitude, then release them, much like they still do today. I remember there was a winch attached to a motor near the front fence that had a cable stretched out along the runway, and it was used to pull the gliders down the runway. As they got overhead, it would release them, then the cable would again be stretched out along the runway to take another one up. I do not know how successful it was, and at what altitude they were released. I don't think it was used very often, maybe because it just did not work very well. The glider club moved somewhere north of Dallas and is still in operation in Midlothian, Texas.

The Korean War broke out in 1950, and the plant was off and running again. The production of a new fighter, the F4U Corsair fighter. The Marine Corps then had Vought to build one designed for them. The AU-1 was used by them for air-to-ground support. Then, in June 1950, the plant merged with James Ling, an electronics firm. It then operated as Ling Temco Vought (LTV).

Aviation has been very important to the growth of Grand Prairie, and likewise, Grand Prairie was very important during the war effort. Anyone who worked at the plant during the war can be proud of what was accomplished during those times.

Soon after the war in 1945, the Moody brothers bought some surplus machinery from TEMCO and began building aluminum boats using similar technology that was used to build aircraft for the war effort. Aluminum was riveted to form the boats. I remember the boats became known worldwide, and it was very successful. They actually helped put Grand Prairie on the map.

I remember seeing a newsreel at the movie theater, and there was a Lone Star Boat on a riverbank in Africa, and I realized then how important that plant was. It was bought and sold several times, and in 1962, a new plant was built in Plano, Texas. It became a large employer for the citizens there. Then, in 1965, Chrysler Boats was formed, and they bought the plant in Plano to build a new kind of boat. The fiberglass-constructed boats were a brand-new technology, and this became a large employer for Plano, Texas. The brochures that were printed in 1966 advertised "Lone Star & Chrysler," but in 1967, they dropped the "Lone Star" and became simply Chrysler Marine. They went on to make fiberglass motorboats and sailboats of all sizes. They later bought out West Bend Outboards, and Chrysler Outboard was born.

POEMS FROM THE PEN OF YOURS TRULY

I had written poems off and on throughout my life, but never saved most of them. A few years ago, I made a notebook and stuck them in there. I reread them later and started writing as a hobby. I also took a writing class and realized I really did enjoy writing. The type of poetry I write is a form of free verse, and I really just try to tell a story. Some of these are from assignments for the writing class. I also like to write short stories and will relate some here.

For some reason, I started using a header for all my poems and short stories, and it goes like this:

FROM THE PEN OF

Charles Allumbaugh
Class of 1958

Some of my earlier poems that I kept were about my motorcycle, a 2002 Harley-Davidson Fat Boy.

My Harley

It was noon
I was running down the asphalt
The sun was high and bright
The Harley was purring like a kitten at 65 mph
As I moved up past 80 it was humming along
When I passed 100 it was singing a song
but the song it was singing was
Just a Closer Walk with Thee
So
I slowed back down so I could hear it purring again

I rode the Harley for several years and enjoyed every minute of it, but eventually sold it, knowing I was pushing my luck. My family thought I was getting too old to ride — maybe they were right.

THE YEAR WAS 1953

The story begins...
In a time and galaxy that seems so far away, there was a kid that heard of a new kind of car in the showroom at Graff Chevrolet in Grand Prairie, Texas.
He walked the two miles or so from 1621 Willow Street in the Fairview addition in Grand Prairie to see what they were talking about.

*He stood outside that window looking at a brand new 1953 and ½
Chevrolet Corvette Convertible.*

*He knew right then that someday he was going to own one of those
Corvettes. When he turned 65, he bought his first Harley-Davidson
(not his first motorcycle), a Fat Boy.*

Years later, after selling the Harley, I set out on a new adventure
to make that Corvette dream a reality.

Even though I had a three-car garage, one side was completely
full of tools. I did not have a place to put my tools and riding
mower, so I set out to do something about it. I took all the money
I got for the Harley and started a remodel. I had a tool shed built
in the backyard. I moved everything I could out to that tool shed
and put some in the attic. Then I repainted the garage and cleaned
it up.

All this took several weeks, and everyone asked me when I was
going to buy that car. No one in my family thought I was going to
do it because they had heard me talk about it for years. Even some
of my neighbors would come over and ask where the car was.

I set out on the internet to learn all about the different models
and why the different prices when they all looked the same on the
outside.

I went to *Gurus.com* and started looking for the right one. I
would find one that sounded promising and drag my wife along
to look at it. We drove cars from Tyler, Texas, to Weatherford. I
found one in Weatherford that I liked, but my wife did not think
it was the one. She was right again. Go figure.

I finally found one in Rockwall, Texas, that I liked. After I test
drove it, I knew it was the one. I made an offer to Jason, the sales-
man, and he said that he could not take it to his boss because it
was just too low. Go figure. I insisted, and he did. He returned with

the second rung up the ladder (every dealer has one). He said that they could not sell the car for that and made a counteroffer. I said, even though that car only has 3,915 miles on it, it was still nearly four years old. He looked right back and said, "YEP." I knew right then if I wanted that car, I had to pay the price they were asking. I am now 77 years old, and I feel like that kid back in 1953 looking through the window of Graff Chevrolet.

When I got home with the new car, I wrote several poems about the Corvette.

THE C7

I was running down the interstate
460 horses under the hood
I looked in the rearview and what did I see
The Ellis County sheriff was a-coming for me
I laid down on the gas pedal
But he was still in my rearview and still after me
He don't get paid enough to stay up with me
As I pushed a little harder
I saw him trailing
But not so close
Then I heard a funny sound
Coming from above
Oh Lordy
That chopper was just so close to me
I was running out of road
I shoulda stayed on that Interstate 20
I pulled on over
And now what did I see

But that Ellis County sheriff
That was earlier after me
He said, "Well now boy
What do you have to say?"

And all I could think was,
"Watcha want with me?"

THE BEST HIGH OF ALL

Some people get high on marijuana
Some get high on beer
Me, I just get high riding my C7 all the way to here
You got to go with me
Let me show you my high
I think you will love it just like I do my dear
If you think that Mustang your driving
Is the cat's meow
Come with me in this piece of heaven
That's what I call my C7
This 'Vette is fast with a heat shield up front
That's what it takes to keep burning up this road
I hope these tires are not too slick
Cause I can't afford to slip and slide with all the smoke we'll make
See that Porsche car in front
He's a fixing to see my tail lights and
Just the rear end of me
Oh I'm riding high and feeling mighty fine
Even with that highway patrol who's following behind
Let's see what this C7 will do

And show him a thing or two
Yippie-yi-yay all the way
Here we come Sante Fe
El Paso just passed us on the left
Have I already said, "Here we come Sante Fe!"

BIG SHOT HENRY

Big shot Henry
With his 460 Hemi
It had four in the floor
And four-wheel drive
It was built by Henry
when he was still alive
He knew how to drive it
And drove all the girls wild
Then one day after
A hard night a drinking
Along came Suzie
As cute as she could be
She was driving a
Four in the floor '58 Chevy
They just stared at each other
Not saying a word
Both knew what was
A fixin' to happen
They lined up on Highway 80
The hoods were shaking
The exhaust was smoking
And the race was on

After the first bend
Ol' Henry was way out ahead
Then the '58 Chevy
Got it's second wind
Another curve was coming up
But Ol' Henry just wouldn't let up
Suzie saw what was going to take place
Ol' Henry was going to really lose this race
She tried to warn him
But he wouldn't listen
The curve was just too close
Henry sailed off the end
He just waved goodbye
with that silly Henry grin

THE QUICK STOP

Well! I took her out early one morning
I can still hear those tailpipes a-rumblin'
I made a quick stop at the local QUICK STOP
And filled her up with that tier one petrol
I cleaned the windshield and checked the oil
I put the hose back in the pump
As I stood the pattin' the hood
Right between the headlights I stood
I was supposed to head right back home
I guess 'cause I told her I would
Just one more run down 287 won't take but a minute
I knew I could
But before I knew it I passed the city limit sign

All the traffic I had left behind
I headed on out to the toll road so I told myself I could turn around
But I hit the gas
Oklahoma…here I come!
This C7 is really bright red
When the phone rang I knew I was dead
I answered the phone and quickly I said
I told her I was on 287 and would be home in a minute or so
I passed the Oklahoma Panhandle
I don't remember Amarillo a short time ago
I knew I should head home as I was told
She already knew I had lied again
But this time I could not blame it on my best friend Ben
He had covered for me every now and then
I know I can turn around when I leave that little town known as Cheyenne
Cause that's where you hit Highway 80 also known as the Highway to Heaven
And this C7 is the best way to get there

The Book of Life

The book of life
Has already been written
How many pages
it holds is unknown
How many days to a page
Is determined by how we live

The Wooster Rooster

There was a man from Wooster
He cut off the head of his rooster
When ask about the deed
he boasted
His rooster had already been roasted

The Ring

The ring I put on your finger
No end shall it have
Just round and round in life
May it go on forever

I also wrote some really short poems I call truisms.

The Two of Us in Three Words

You
Me
We

One Week Without Prayer

Makes one weak

Hidden in Every Piece of Marble

Is a masterpiece

Sometimes Memories Are All We Have Left

Cherish them forever
As we grow old, they will comfort us

Why

Don't you love me like I love you

Sand

Like the sands of time
You slipped thru my fingers

May Your Best Luck

Always be on your
windward side

A Question of Evidence

With all the evidence
Before you
Would you still vote the same

The Angel in You

The angel in you shined so bright
The devil in me took such delight

At the End of the Rainbow

I will wait for you

There Are Reasons Why

There are times to behold
Call for reason
Call for truth
Show respect
Show you care
Give It Your Best Shot
Give it your best shot
No matter what life brings

Give it your best shot
Even on the small things
Give it your best shot
For all to see
Give it your best shot
For all you can be

Some of the poems and short stories came from my writers' class, and some are just about some type of holiday. This next one is a short story about Thanksgiving.

Thanksgiving at Maudes

I think I'll just sit out here on this porch
And hold Maude's baby
Kinda watch and see how everyone drives up

Maude had kids almost grown
When this baby came along
Kinda unexpected like but
Will just loves him to death
Maude didn't want another one
With all the others 'bout growed up and all
But I guess she didn't know what caused the other three
Billy Sue was already in High School
And was embarrassed
In front of all her classmates
That her mother and dad was doing what caused it
Schucks I still–Hmm– well I won't go there

Here comes Phil and Laura Lee and her brood
She married a black guy from Houston
Everyone was kinda shocked when she did but
He seems nice and now fits right in
Him and Maude's husband goes fishing together
C'ause he's the one with a boat I guess
Seems to have a really good job
But has to drive back and forth to work in Houston
Promised Laura Lee she could stay here
Since she had family and all
32 miles one way in traffic
But he drives a Corvette
And said it was his quiet time
Here comes Bess and her husband
They couldn't have kids you know
She always talked about having
Kids of her own when we was in High School
That's the way it always seems to be I guess
The ones that want something the most
They drive a big Cadillac and go overseas a lot

I'll say here comes Trudy
She missed the last year or two
With all those babies in the car I can see why
Bob—That's her husband you know —
Was in the war and they say he has PTSD or something like that
Never could get that just right
He's kinda quiet about it so no one ask what it was like
Maude's husband and Phil tried to get him to go deer hunting
But he just said he didn't like guns

But he does go fishing with them
They seem to like being together
I never did like guns myself so
I can understand it.

Well, I do declare
Here comes Paul and his new wife
No one has met her yet
Hear she's kinda young for him
We all wondered who would marry dear old Paul
We joke about him behind his back
But I guess he's really ok
He finished high school then went to Harvard
Got some kind of degree in something
And now teaches at the university
He always was kind weird about politics and all
We try to not get him started on it
But it seems something can always set him off

Well, it's almost time for dinner
So, I guess I better help set the table
Babies asleep now and if I'm real quiet
I can put him in his crib

The next one is about Christmas. But it is not your normal Christmas story. I always try to write something different from the norm.

Did Santa Stop By Your House Last Night

Did Santa stop by your house last night
I was sitting on the porch steps
Just thinking about you
When I thought I saw Santa
With that red coat on
Your lights turned down
It was hard to see
But you know
I sure thought I saw Santa
at your house last night
Was that his red sleigh
In your driveway
I sure thought
I saw Santa at your house last night
I missed you at the park
Did you miss me too
I sure thought I saw Santa
at your house last night.
You know if your ever lonely
You can count on me
Now tell me right
Tell me true
Was that really Santa
at your house last night

The Picture in the Paper

I saw your picture in the paper this morning
I've seen it there before
When we graduated and thought we were on the top of the world
And then when we went to college and thought we would never part
But life stepped in and we did
We went our separate way
Your wedding day was there
And when your kids were born
Everything you did it seems, with your picture there to see
I always wondered if you ever thought of me
I was sorry to hear that Bob passed away
You know I knew him from the old neighborhood
I saw you at his funeral but you never saw me
It didn't seem the proper time to stop and say hello
I still wondered if you ever thought of me
As I put away the paper I heard a knock
And I opened up the door
A young man stood there looking back at me
As he introduced himself I said yes I know who you are
I guess you heard that mom passed away
She often talked of you
All the things you did and the fun you had
She missed those times
I could tell she thought a lot of you
As she lay there dying
She made a request you see
She wanted you to help carry her
To her final resting place
She thought that much of you

I saw your picture in the paper this morning
I've seen it there before

This next one I wrote as a prayer. I asked the class if they had ever written something funny and even laughed out loud while writing it. Most said yes. I then asked if they had ever written something so sad that they actually had a tear in their eye while they wrote it. No one had. One of the ladies said, "Oh no…we are going home on a sad note?"

It is titled, *Hello Lord.*

Hello Lord

Well hello Lord
You know
I never ask you for much
But it seems
I can't do this one alone
I don't go to church
I never ask a lot of questions
I never thought I would
But it seems Lord
I can't figure a way
To do this one alone
You know Lord
You would think
If you loved someone enough
There would be nothing
You couldn't do
But it seems Lord

That I need your help
Just this one time
I never thought I would
If there is anything
You want of me
Just say it
And I will promise you
If you just help me now
There is nothing I wouldn't do
I kneel on bended knee
And ask you Lord
Just hear my plea
I sit beside the one I loved
Her breathing is so shallow
I am scared Lord
I don't know what to do
Please just hear my prayer Lord
And there's nothing I won't do

Angel Wings

So many songs have been written
About doves
and wings
And angels
And other things
To try to understand
What they all mean
Is difficult you see
For me at least

So when dove wings sound
The air moves
The angels fly
And love abounds
For me at least
So many songs about all
These things
Are still unwritten
So let your imagination
Determine the meaning
About dove wings and angels
And love
And other things

Gimme A Do-Over

Well, I been thinking
That's hard I know
What would life be like
If I had a do-over
I tried and I tried
To think about this
This is all I could
come up with
I know it's kinda crazy
But here it is
If I had a do-over
I'd look like Alan Jackson
Wearing that
White cowboy hat

If I had a do over
I'd kinda sing like Alan Jackson
With that white cowboy hat
You think I'm obsessed
Well not really
I can imagine
What he has gone thru
That guitar strumming
And that white hat shining
That mustache never needing trimming
The songs that he sung
And the stages he's been on
I think I might
Just be able to get along
Well now that I thought
And I thought on this
I had a pretty good run
And about all the things I'd miss
The kids and grandkids too
Oh yes, the great ones too
I think I'll just stay with what I got
Look like Alan Jackson and sing like Alan Jackson
Hmmm! let me just give it some thought

The next poem is about a pecan tree.

The Pecan Tree

At the front of the chapel
Sat a lonely wooden casket

He had made it
With his own two hands
* He had made it for him to use*
He never thought she would need it first
* He made it from the wood*
Of the old pecan tree
* The one he had planted*
When they first got married
* The old pecan tree*
Was only 80 years old
* It withered and died*
Way before it's time
* Sometimes life is like that*
Whether you are human
* Or just a old pecan tree*
That died before it's time
* It took ten years*
For that old pecan tree to bear its first fruit
* The ones*
We would harvest each fall
* That old pecan tree*
Had hardly started to grow
* When the first child came along*
It was a big bouncing boy
* We were so proud of him*
He was born in the fall
* Like the first fruit*
Of that old pecan tree
* Then along came the girl*
My pride and joy
* We watched them both grow*

So tall and straight
  And just like the pecan tree
They grew and grew
  I remember sitting
Under that old tree
  Watching the kids
As they played and they played
  Their mother was so proud
Of both of them
  They grew into fine adults
And started their own families
  Then something happened
To that old pecan tree
  It withered and died
Kinda unexpectedly
  And in our twilight years
We knew our time was close
  I cut that old pecan tree down
And made lumber from it
  And made that casket
For me to use
  Why was I left here all alone
Just looking at that casket
  The one we had grown
From a sapling
  Then I remembered
The old pecan tree as it grew
  And the kids also
Watched it grow
  Everything and everyone has its time
And I had mine

Someday we'll be together again
But for now, I have those memories
    Of her
And that old pecan tree

Times Forgotten

Now as I sit in this garden
So peaceful and quiet
    I look at your tombstone
So gray and so lonely
    I know that someday we will be
Side by side again
    The rose I brought
Will be wilted and dried
    I remember the times
That we laughed and we cried
    When the children came
It was the best of times
    Those times remembered
Those times forgotten

There is no subject that you cannot write about. The next one is about the wind.

The Wind

Do you hear the wind
Do you feel it now

It blows so softly
Against the trees
The leaves slowly move and they
Remind me of you
The movement is so sensuous
And daring
It is as if you are causing them to move about
So softly and quiet
It completely surrounds us now
Can you feel it as it pulses against us
The slight push of the air
As it nudges against us
The wind is picking up now
Can you feel it as it gains strength
What was a moment ago
So soft and quiet
Is now beginning to overpower us
And control my very thought of you
The thought of you is what I have missed
As I try to remember your every movement
I miss you and this wind is just a reminder
Of what you were like
You were like the wind
And I will never ever lose that thought of you

One of our assignments in the writing class was to write about
the phrase, "The wind through the willows moans like an Irish
banshee." This is what I came up with:

What is that sound
I hear it so clearly
It moans like a banshee
From Eire
What is that sound
I hear it so clearly
Maybe it's my Aoife
My lady from Eire
I know what it is
The moaning from Eire
It sings thru the willows
Like an Irish banshee

My beautiful angel
My Irish lass
'Tis no banshee after all
Just my Aoife singing to me

Seasons

The seasons change
They come and go
Spring then summer then fall

But the best season of all is winter
The season of Thanksgiving
For the birth of the Christ child is near

Christmas is for all
The children laugh and play
Wishing for Christmas to come

Sometimes we forget
What Christmas is for
But celebrate the time with family
It's also that time of year

Skipping Rocks

Life is like that you see
Sometimes you sink
and sometimes you don't
Sometimes you just bounce along
Life is like that you see
Just like skipping rocks
The smoother the water
the further you can go
just like skipping rocks
When the water is rough
The harder it is
Then you can sink
Just like skipping rocks
Then someone
Comes along and
picks you up again
Giving you another chance
To just skip along

The Rose in Your Garden

As I lay awake and I
Looked out the window
I could see the rose in your garden
As by the moonlight it
Shined so bright
It reminded me of you
Then as the morning light
Came peeking above the cloudy sky
I saw the sun light up that rose
And it shined so bright it reminded me of you
I planted that rose and you never knew
You wondered where it came from
And it shined so bright it reminded me of you
I picked that rose this morning
And took it with me to the Chapel
As I walked to the front of the church
And I placed it beside you
It shined so bright it reminded me of you
Then the sky started to rumble and the
Dark clouds covered the sun
As we walked up the hill
To your final resting place
The light broke thru and there on you casket
Lay a single red rose
That shined so bright
It reminded me of you

Halloween: A Day at the Park

The Witches and Goblins and Devils too
All gathered around the kid on the trike
His brother on his bike had gone on ahead
Out of his sight he could not be seen
He didn't what to do
So, he peddled and peddled as fast as he could
The Witches and Goblins and the Devil too
Just followed him and chased him all the way the park
But it was already getting dark, he just didn't know what to do
He knew he had to take a stand, but could he really
Then all of a sudden there was a big noise
His brother was there and ran them all off
Those Witches and Goblins and the Devil too
All disappeared and he was saved
For that's what big brothers do

Valentine

What is a Valentine

Is it the card you got
Either in person or in the mail
Or is it like my Valentine
The girl next door
Or down the street
Remember all the kids
On the block where you lived
There were more in my short block

Than any I can remember

Let's see now there was
Truman
Joe Dean
Jerry Don
Phillip
David
Johnny
Bobby
Allen
Judy
Max
Jerry
Billy
The Messick brothers
Then there was Gay (boy) Kay (girl) who were twins
Couple of others that moved away I don't remember their names
Most were boys and the girls were too young to play with us boys
We all played Annie over
Kick the can
Cops and robbers
Cowboys and Indians
All day long until it got dark
And even after
We didn't have time for girls
Until 1946 when I started the 1st grade
At Williams B Travis grade school
Low and behold
The class was full of all things
GIRLS

When Valentine's Day came along
Everyone traded Valentine cards
With little sayings on them
The cutest girl in the class brought me hers
And it opened up and said
I love you with a big red heart
I was embarrassed
That the cutest girl in the class
Said that to little old me
The only thing was
She gave every boy and girl in the class the same card with the same
saying.
I only found that out much later
Jeez! What a bummer
She could have been my very own
Valentine but wasn't

Halloween Queen (The Apple of My Eye)

It's not black or white
It's black and orange
It started with love
And ended in fear
My Halloween Queen
That's who I mean
I met her in the graveyard
The one on lonely road
Down by the boondocks

Where the railroad tracks end
She flew in on a broomstick
And swept me off my feet
This Halloween Queen
I'll describe her to you
Her hair was jet black
And her teeth were orange
Her eyes glowed in the dark
As her arms reached for me
The fear came over me
I couldn't move
I knew I was a goner
This was a nightmare for me
Then as I opened my eyes
The pillow was all wet
The Halloween Queen
Was only a dream

We had another subject to write about that I had never thought about, and that was to write about a were-animal. We had all heard of a "werewolf," but this was supposed to be a different kind. This is what I came up with.

WereRabbit

Well, we have all heard
Of a werewolf
Scary as it is

But did you ever
Hear of a wererabbit
Well, a wererabbit
You see is nothing like a werewolf
Well for the most part
He ain't
He can throw up a curse
Or hide in a briar patch
Much like old
Brer Rabbit
Used to do
But Brer Rabbit
He ain't
He's as opposite
As he can be
He's not for little kiddies
Or even for you or me
He can grow as big as a giant
Or hide in the palm of your hand
So, if you don't
Believe in him
Then don't
And maybe
Just maybe
He will leave
you alone

MY DAD'S PART IN SHAPING
THE SKYLINE OF DALLAS

M y dad was a journeyman electrician and neon sign worker. He was the Job foreman on the Mercantile Bank Tower, which was completed in 1947. You could see the tower from my home in Grand Prairie, Texas. At that time, it was the tallest structure west of the Mississippi River. The light from the neon would flow up or down the sign, and depending on which way it flowed, you could tell whether the temperature was going up or down. I remember he came home one day and said he dropped his billfold from the top of one of the towers. The last he saw of it, it was going out of sight and heading towards the sidewalk below.

He was the shop foreman for another company that built the Tower on the Republic Bank building, which surpassed the height of the Mercantile Bank tower. It was said they actually added the tower just so they could be the tallest building, surpassing the Mercantile Bank tower. It was completed in 1954.

I believe those two towers still stand atop both buildings. I realize now how important a part he played in the history of Dallas and helped to shape the skyline of Dallas. You could also see the Flying Red Horse on top of the Mobile building from my front yard. At some point, I believe he was involved in a repair on the sign.

There were many other neon signs around Dallas that he did the layout for. One such sign was in front of all the Skillern's Drug Stores. It stood on top of a large concrete pedestal in front of each store.

MORE OF MY WRITINGS

This short story I wrote is titled *Avoid the Cliche*.

It was a dark and stormy night. The old house creaked and groaned as the storm battered the outside. Genevieve closed and secured the last shutter, then lowered the sash and locked the window. As she settled down in front of the fireplace, she tucked her feet under her and wrapped her husband's old flannel robe tightly around her.

He had only been gone two years, and she still missed him. Fido was his dog and now hers. Why Fido, well, why not? It is a good old Italian name and one of the oldest names for dogs in all of history. Spot would not work because he doesn't have any spots. Besides, Abraham Lincoln's dog was named Fido, and what was good enough for Honest Abe was good enough for her.

She had given away most of his clothes, but could not give his flannel robe away. When she wrapped it around her, she could feel him and smell his scent.

The same was with his dog. She had never particularly liked the dog, but now realized she could never part with him. He was always company, and she knew he would protect her with his life. It did seem that he knew Ken was not coming back, and he transferred his loyalty to her. It was obvious at first that the dog missed him, but sensed that he knew she missed him too.

As the dark night surrounded the house, the storm was growing in intensity. The lightning was also intense, as was the thunder that accompanied it. The fire was comforting, as was the dog and the robe. They helped drown out what was going on just outside the window.

All of a sudden, lightning struck the hundred-year-old oak tree in front of the dining room window, causing it to split down the middle and crash through the roof into the dining room.

The cat was asleep under the window and screeched loudly. He was trapped under a large limb and could not get out from under it.

The dog amazingly woke up, ran to the room, and pulled the limb back with his teeth. She had never seen an animal react in such a manner. He and the cat had been friendly towards each other for several years, and his instincts just took over, and he saved the cat from further injury.

She had heard of dogs reacting in a similar manner while protecting a child, but never another animal.

She knew that Ken had left a gift that she would always be thankful for.

Dreams

When I dream the dreams of life and death
And all the times in between

I mostly dream the dreams of you with me
I wonder when we pass from this earth
If our dreams will pass with us
Of all the dreams I will carry with me
The dream of life with you
Is the dream I would choose
There are glad dreams and sad dreams
Blue dreams and red dreams
And dreams of all the colors of the rainbow
The best dreams have no color at all
Just memories with us together
Forever and ever

Songs Still Unwritten

So many songs
have been written
About doves
and wings
And Angels
and other things
To try to understand
What they all mean
Is difficult
You see
For me at least
So when dove wings sound
The air moves
The angels fly
And love abounds

For me at least
To try to understand
What it all means
Is difficult
You see
For me at least
So many songs
About all these things
Are still unwritten
So let your imagination
Determine the meaning
About dove wings
And Angels
And love
And other things

Times Forgotten

Now as I sit in this garden
So peaceful and quiet
I look at your tombstone
So gray and so lonely
I know that someday we will be
Side by side
I remember the times
That we laughed and we cried
When the children came it was the best of times
Those times remembered and
Those times forgotten

THE MOVIE BUSINESS IN GRAND PRAIRIE

S ome of my favorite memories had to be at the local theatres. The Uptown Theatre opened March 17,1950, as an un-segregated theatre years before others would follow. The theatre was actually still segregated, with blacks in the balcony and whites on the first floor. There was also a small stage where live performances took place.

But the Wings Theatre was where we all met every Saturday Morning. We would watch the serials, and we had to go back each Saturday morning to see what would happen in the next episode. Red Rider and his companion Little Beaver, Whip Wilson, Lash Larue, the Lone Ranger, Buck Rogers, Adventures of Captain Marvel, Superman, The Green Hornet, Bat Man, Sky King, Roy Rogers, Hopalong Cassidy with his white horse Topper, Wild Bill Hickok, Captain Midnight, Our Gang and my favorite, Flash Gordon Conquers the Universe were just a few that we watched.

The Shadow always started off with, "What lies behind the creaking door? Only the shadow knows."

In 1948, Jerry Silvers and his brother Sherman moved to Grand Prairie, Texas, and, along with his sister, Helen Meager Fisher, went into the picture show business. They had been in the theatre business in Minnesota and liked the possibilities of going into the theatre business in Grand Prairie. They bought the Wings theatre and rented the Texas theatre across the street. Then, in 1950, they opened a brand new 1000-seat Uptown Theatre. It was very modern for its time. I remember it had a double seat for large customers, but the seat was popular for a boy and a girl to sit together. There was also a glassed-in cry room for mothers with crying babies. It was also popular for boys and girls to use. Fancy that. There was also a smoking section for smokers.

I, along with 10 or 12 other boys, would deliver show circulars every other Saturday. We would pile into the back of two pickup trucks and deliver a circular to every house in Grand Prairie. It would take about two hours, and then we would go back to the Uptown Theatre, and Jerry would pay us with a Coke and popcorn or a candy bar. Then we would get free show tickets to see upcoming movies.

I remember standing in line while Jerry poured Cokes for us, and he turned and asked me my name. I told him Allumbaugh, and he said, "Do you know what that stands for in German?" Of course, I said no, and he said, "Tree Branch." Then he turned and finished serving our drinks. When I got home, I told my dad what he said, and he just laughed. Of course, Jerry was just making fun of me, and I fell for it.

Tickets were 35 cents, and children's tickets were 12 cents. It is said that Jerry Silver's mother invented the pickle juice snow cone, and it was popular with some. There was also an Old Maid bag of popcorn that used half-popped kernels. Jerry's mother was very frugal and probably invented both. I always thought both were awful.

During the 1950s, parents would drop off their small children to see the kiddie shows at the Uptown, but the Wings Theatre was where us older kids would go.

They also had a midnight movie for the employees of the aircraft plant who worked the late shift.

I wrote the following poem about the Wings Theatre.

What A Shame

There are people being born today
That may never hear Johnny Cash
Or Loretta Lynn or George Jones
Or Brenda Lee
What a shame

These same people being born today
Will never understand
How great John Wayne was
And how tall he was in the saddle
What a shame

To go back to the Wings Theatre
On Saturday morning
And watch the serials with Whip Wilson
And Lash LaRue or Flash Gordon
Who are they you say. What' a serial
Oh wow. What a shame

Flash Gordon, What a memory
"Flash Gordon Conquers the Universe"
Oh man if you could not experience that
What a shame
Then we would lay in front of the big Admiral radio
And make believe we were part of the story
The Green Hornet and Stella Dallas
Stella who you say, Oh wow
What a shame
We would go to bed that night and have nightmares about
"What lies behind the creaking door"
You cannot imagine that you say
What a shame

We never dreamed of a computer or an iPad or an iPhone
But we knew the concept of an Apple watch
Because Dick Tracy had one
Who's Dick Tracy you say
Oh wow I give up
What a shame

It's Just a Fable

Well it's just a fable
Not true, but made up

So read it at your leisure
It will entertain you

The following is just made up
But it could have been true

So settle down in comfort
And here it is for you

Little Red Riding Hood
Was running from the law
She has brought along her companions

Miss Piggy and her three cousins
Little pigs that come in threes
Mo and Curly and Jack

They robbed a bank in Tucson
And thought they had it made

Then as they passed that billboard
A siren they did hear
It was loud and screeching
In all of their ears

Then as they gained on the law behind them
He was getting smaller in their rearview

Then up above them
They heard this awful noise

The bullets in front of them
Did straif the concrete highway

So little Red Riding Hood
Slowed to a crawl

That Dallas County Sheriff
With a big grin on his face

That earlier was so far behind them
On his motorcycle and all

Said well well now
Ain't it a shame

Little Red Riding Hood
Couldn't think of what to say

So this came out of her mouth
As she batted her eyes at him

Watch'a want with little Ole' Me'

The Pine Box

The old pine box sat at the front of the church
He sat at the back
His whole life sat there before him
All the memories sat there too
Why was it that he was still here and his whole life seemed gone
As he sat there and reflected on all the good times
He remembered how the gray skies would open up
and turn into a gentle falling rain

And the times they would sit on the porch
and reflect on how life had been so good
And how the porch swing slowly turned to a gently
rocking chair that they both enjoyed so much
The kids all grew up and left our home to take
Their turn to make a home of their own
Now the old pine box looks so lonely as it sits
In front of this old country church
I'll be with you again someday

The Old Rocking Chair

I remember the nights
I remember them well
I watched you in the old rocking chair

The sewing kit sat by your side
I remember so well I can't forget
The kids as you rocked them to sleep
Oh I remember it all
The rocking chair
It still sits where you left it
I can't bring myself
to move it from there

Oh I remember the nights
You rocked and rocked
So slowly it seemed the rhythm
Of the old rocking chair

The kids are all grown
But the memories still there
I will always remember you
And that old rocking chair

Logan and His Horse

Wild horses wild horses
They will run from you
But tame them and train them
And they will love you true
To love an animal so big and so strong
He will always try to please you and do no wrong
What a pleasure it is to saddle him up
And ride out to the pasture
Just like the girl last Saturday night
He will waltz with you if you treat him right
He will run into a herd of Brahma Bulls
And if your not careful make a fool of you
For he shows no fear when they are near
But your heart is beating and you lungs full of air
With others around they look and stare
With that rope in your hand he will chase that steer
And show disappointment when you miss the mark
But will do it again until you ask him to quit
He knows he is part of the show
He will perform
There you go you missed again

He sometimes turns his head
And looks at you in wonderment
But does your bidding and will do it again
Until you again ask him to quit

It's Hard to Be A Cowboy

Well it's hard to be a cowboy
This day and time

Riding and roping and
Singing those songs

Well it's hard to be a cowboy
This day and time

Singing yippie – i – a
And riding along

Well it's hard to be a cowboy
This day and time
The West Texas towns
Are still far and wide

The trails are much smaller
So traveled they are

It takes horses and cattle
And old blue hounds

And campfires at dusk
With the moon and stars beginning to show

It takes cowgirls and cowboys
And their kids all together

The nights are long as they dream of the times
And what could have been

Oh it's hard to be a cowboy
But if we stay together

Those dreams of the times
Will live within us forever

Just Two Guys Talking - Birthday Blues

What day is this

Why it's Tuesday of course

No! I mean what day is this

Hmm! Well I say it's Tuesday
Yesterday was Monday
Tomorrow is Wednesday
So today is Tuesday

I know it's Tuesday
but that's not what I meant

Well you ask me what day it is
but you won't listen when I tell you it's Tuesday

I know fool that today is Tuesday
But I don't mean what day of the week this is

Well what do you want me to say if you don't
Want me to say it's Tuesday

I just wanted you to tell me what day this is
It's my birthday that's what day it is

Well how was I to know this was your birthday
For goodness sake. Happy birthday then

Wow finally

Seven Angels

All you got to do
Is lean against a tree
Along the muddy banks
Of the Mississippi
Take out you Bible
Turn to the Good Book
To the book of Revelation
What you were supposed to see
In the Good Book
And the book of Revelation
The last book of the Bible

You see
It tells about the slaves
And the hell that awaits
About the seven angels
As they blow their trumpets
For all to hear
The sounds of their wings
As they descend from the heavens
The more you read
Of the book of Revelation
You will understand
The lucky number seven
And why it is so
Slavery didn't start in this country
Because it has always been
We are slaves of God
Jehovah be it so

The Leaves of Fall

The golden leaves of fall
The trees of winter then lose them all
The chlorophyll of spring brings
Them back to life again
Summer holds them to life till the
Golden leaves of fall return again

A Different Light

Some see the world in a different light
I know I do
Do you

Don't hit the switch
Keep it bright
It's hard to see
Without the light

As we get old the light may dim
You still find truth and light thru him
When you are young you do not feel
The times pass by

But pass it does and
The time will come while looking back
You shake your head
And wonder where it all has gone

To be eighteen again would seem so great
But then you realize
All the things you'd have to do all over again
Maybe I'll just stay where I am

This is where I was meant to be
Along with you and our family

Reasons to Believe

When I look at the
Moon and Stars
And all the heavens above
I have reasons to believe

When I look at the
Green green grass
And the tall tall trees
I have reasons to believe

When I look at the rivers
And the quiet mountain streams
And the babbling brooks
I have reasons to believe

When I look at the oceans
And the seas of the earth
And all the life within
I have reasons to believe

Then I read of all the wars
And death from evil
And the sickness that God has brought
Do I have reasons to believe

With the rise and fall of nations
The wars that mankind has wrought
And the storms that God has brought
Do I have reasons to believe

When I look at the children
That came after me
The grandkids and the
Great grandkids then and only then
Do I have a reason to believe

I grew up in the 40s with a lot of good friends. There are not many of us left. I try to call each one and check on them. Not enough, I am sure. The next poem touches on this and covers the period from the 40s to today.

I used to get my Cherry Cokes
At the Dairy Queen on Main

My hamburgers at Gordon's and the
Prairie Dog across town

The Big Boy served breakfast
It was all that you could eat

Graff was where you bought your Chevrolet
And Stolz Motors was for Ford

Murphy Sinclair on the east end of Main
Coker's on the west

The competition was strong
And they stayed the best of friends

Can you imagine what it would be
If they had it to to do over again

Randall Edwards used to set pins
At the local Bowling Alley

Charles MacKenzie was a clown
At The Wings on Saturday morning

He and Jerry Silvers
Could put on a very good show

The old gang that used to play
On Willow Street is all scattered now

Some have passed on to another world
To wait for us to catch up with them

Some have borne illnesses that we never
Would have imagined, but we trudge on

We all had kids
and then they had theirs

Life has been great
No matter the problems

Thru sad times and bad times
We persevere

See you down the road
We will meet again no doubt to be true

I have enjoyed taking the time to write this and hope you enjoyed reading it. There was no way to print all the poems that my grandmother and I wrote.

I hope that she would be pleased to know that some of her stuff was published so others could enjoy them. There was no way at 15 or 16 years old, in the year 1879 or 80, that she would have dreamed this could happen.

I have said that the only real time machine may be a book. I have read her poems and even touched the same pencil lead that she touched over a hundred and 45 years ago. Now I can send it into the future for someone else to read.

Thanks again for taking the time to read this. I will finish this up with one last poem of mine and one of my Grandmother's.

Sorry Not Today

I wrote you a letter
But I never heard from you
I waited and then I waited
To hear a word from you
I called out to the postman
He just turned and looked at me
His words for me were
Sorry not today
I wrote you a letter
But I never heard from you
Whenever the postman comes by
He just turns and says
Sorry not today
I just hope that you're not lonely

As I am today
I'll write another letter
And hope I hear from you
The postman just went by
and he turned and looked at me
His words were the same as always
Sorry not today

This last poem from my Grandmother seems appropriate to end a book.

53

When on this page
You chance to see
Just think of me
And close the book

NOTES

1   Texas State Historical Association. "Peters Colony." Handbook of Texas Online, https://www.tshaonline.org/handbook/entries/peters-colony.

2   Texas State Historical Association. "Peters Colony." Handbook of Texas Online, https://www.tshaonline.org/handbook/entries/peters-colony.

3   "Peters Colony." Collin County History, www.collincountyhistory.com/peters-colony.html.

4   "Peters Colony." Collin County History, www.collincountyhistory.com/peters-colony.html.

5   Moore, Mamie Yeary, editor. Reminiscences of the Boys in Gray, 1861–1865. Self-published, 1912. Digitized by the Antietam Institute, https://antietaminstitute.org.

6   "Abraham Lincoln and Emancipation" | Articles and Essays | Abraham Lincoln Papers at the Library of Congress |Digital Collections | Library of Congress." The Library of Congress, www.loc.gov/collections/abraham-lincoln-papers/articles-and-essays/abraham-lincoln-and-emancipation.

7   "Bull Run." American Battlefield Trust, www.battlefields.org/learn/civil-war/battles/bull-run.

8   American Battlefield Trust. "Battle of Carthage." Battlefields.org, https://www.battlefields.org/learn/civil-war/battles/carthage.

9   Battle of Fort Sumter, April 1861 (U.S. National Park Service). www.nps.gov/articles/battle-of-fort-sumter-april-1861.htm.

10   "Bull Run." American Battlefield Trust, www.battlefields.org/learn/civil-war/battles/bull-run.

11   Encyclopedia of Arkansas. "USS Tensas." Encyclopedia of Arkansas, July 2024, encyclopediaofarkansas.net/entries/uss-tensas-13723.

12   Encyclopedia of Arkansas. "USS Tensas." Encyclopedia of Arkansas, July 2024, encyclopediaofarkansas.net/entries/uss-tensas-13723.

13   Encyclopedia of Arkansas. "USS Tensas." Encyclopedia of Arkansas, July 2024, encyclopediaofarkansas.net/entries/uss-tensas-13723.

14   Encyclopedia of Arkansas. "USS Tensas." Encyclopedia of Arkansas, July 2024, encyclopediaofarkansas.net/entries/uss-tensas-13723.

15   Encyclopedia of Arkansas. "USS Tensas." Encyclopedia of Arkansas, July 2024, encyclopediaofarkansas.net/entries/uss-tensas-13723.

16   "The Last Battle of the Civil War: Palmito Ranch." Texas State Historical Association, www.tshaonline.org/handbook/entries/palmito-ranch-battle-of.

17   "The Last Battle of the Civil War: Palmito Ranch." Texas State Historical Association, www.tshaonline.org/handbook/entries/palmito-ranch-battle-of.

18   Costa, Barry. "About the Battle." Palmito Ranch Battlefield, 10 June 2020, palmitoranch.cahnr.uconn.edu/about-the-battle.

19   "Twill." Merriam-Webster Dictionary, 26 May 2025, www.merriam-webster.com/dictionary/twill.

20 "Only One Life, Twill Soon Be Past – by C.T. Studd (1860 – 1931)." Reasons for Hope* Jesus, 1 May 2024, reasonsforhopejesus.com/ only-one-life-twill-soon-be-past-by-c-t-studd-1860-1931.

21 Texas State Historical Association. "John Neely Bryan: Founder of Dallas and Indian Trader." Texas State Historical Association, www. tshaonline.org/handbook/entries/bryan-john-neely.

22 Texas State Historical Association. "John Neely Bryan: Founder of Dallas and Indian Trader." Texas State Historical Association, www. tshaonline.org/handbook/entries/bryan-john-neely.

23 https://www.tshaonline.org/handbook/entries/dallas-tx

24 "Starr, Belle." Encyclopedia of Arkansas, June 2024, encyclopediaofarkansas.net/entries/belle-starr-2406.

25 Carthage Female Academy. www.jaspercountyschools.org/ Carthage/id108.htm.

26 Wallis, Michael. "Belle Starr: The Truth Behind the Wild West Legend." Library Journal, www.libraryjournal.com/ review/belle-starr-the-truth-behind-the-wild-west-legend-1815157#:~:text=Her%20brother%20John%20A.M.,to%20 Starr%20and%20her%20family.

27 Goldrush, and Goldrush. "Belle Starr – Outlaw Queen." Nick Brumby Westerns | Unforgettable Western Action Adventures, 6 May 2025, nickbrumbywesterns.com/belle-starr-the-outlaw-queen.

28 "Belle Starr – Outlaw Queen." Nick Brumby Westerns | Unforgettable Western Action Adventures, 6 May 2025, nickbrumbywesterns. com/belle-starr-the-outlaw-queen.

29 Max Bryan Times Record mbryan@swtimes.com. "Fabled Outlaw Belle Starr Tried Twice in Fort Smith." Southwest Times Record, 24 Sept. 2018. www.swtimes.com/story/news/local/2018/09/24/ fabled-outlaw-belle-starr-tried/10181531007.

30 Contest, Fall Writing. "The Ghost of Belle Starr." Short Fiction Break, 22 Nov. 2023, shortfictionbreak.com/the-ghost-of-belle-starr.

31 Encyclopedia of Arkansas. "Starr, Belle." Encyclopedia of Arkansas, June 2024, encyclopediaofarkansas.net/entries/belle-starr-2406/#:~: text=Though%20suspects%20included%20an%20outlaw, today%27s%20Eufaula%20Dam%20in%20Oklahoma.

32 Warfare History Network. "Bushwhackers, Jayhawks, and Red Legs: Missouri's Guerrilla War - Warfare History Network." Warfare History Network, 20 July 2022, warfarehistorynetwork.com/article/ bushwhackers-jayhawks-and-red-legs-missouris-guerrilla-war.

33 "Jayhawkers." Ci Outlaws. www.legendsofamerica.com/we-james youngergang. Civil War on the Western Border, civilwaronthewesternborder.org/encyclopedia/jayhawkers.

34 https://www.historynet.com/james-younger-gang/

35 HISTORY.com Editors. "Jesse James Is Murdered | April 3, 1882 | HISTORY." HISTORY, 25 Jan. 2025, www.history.com/this-day-in-history/april-3/jesse-james-is-murdered.

36 State Fair of Texas. "History | State Fair of Texas." State Fair of Texas, 25 May 2018, bigtex.com/about-us/history.

37 Wikipedia contributors. (2022, May 20). Ross-Johnson RJ-5. Wikipedia. https://en.wikipedia.org/wiki/Ross-Johnson_RJ-5

ACKNOWLEDGMENTS

F irst, I would like to thank my wife for putting up with my need to have a quiet time to write, also for the encouragement from some in my writer's group at the Summit in Grand Prairie, Texas.

It would be impossible to write this type of history without getting a lot of the information from the internet. I would like to thank all those who have posted accounts of the history of some of the famous, or should I say Infamous. I have tried to confirm all the dates listed and hope they are accurate.

A lot of the accounts of the aircraft plant and Lone Star Boats came from my recollection and the internet. The first boat plant was located close to where I lived along Hwy 180 in Grand Prairie, Texas. It was housed in a large metal building.

Some of the accounts of life in Grand Prairie came from my personal memory, and some from the internet.

Again, thank you for reading this.

ABOUT THE AUTHOR

Charles Allumbaugh was born and raised in Grand Prairie, Texas, and graduated from Grand Prairie High School in 1958. He went on to spend thirty-three years with the United States Postal Service, followed by two years of contract work for the Postal Service and five years at Home Depot before fully retiring.

Throughout his life, Charles has enjoyed playing the piano and listening to all kinds of music. He rode motorcycles for about a decade before trading them in for a sports car, which became a favorite hobby.

Later in life, he attended a writing class and discovered his love for poetry and short stories. Inspired by a desire to leave something meaningful behind, Charles decided to write this book. He believes there's no better time machine than a book—you can reach into the past and send it into the future for others to read.

Charles and his wife, Doris, have been married for 65 years. Their long and loving marriage is a foundation for the family stories and legacy shared in this collection.